AF255221

Points, Dots, and Lines

Points, Dots, and Lines

Beauty in the Bible

WILMA ZALABAK

WIPF & STOCK · Eugene, Oregon

POINTS, DOTS, AND LINES
Beauty in the Bible

Wipf & Stock
An Imprint of Wipf and Stock Publishers
199 W. 8th Ave., Suite 3
Eugene, OR 97401

www.wipfandstock.com

PAPERBACK ISBN: 978-1-6667-6620-2
HARDCOVER ISBN: 978-1-6667-6621-9
EBOOK ISBN: 978-1-6667-6622-6

03/21/23

Scripture quotations from the Authorized (King James) Version. Rights in the Authorized Version in the United Kingdom are vested in the Crown. Reproduced by permission of the Crown's patentee, Cambridge University Press.

Some Bible passages are paraphrased by the author of this book, either to summarize and shorten the quotation or to update the tone and vernacular for a character in conversation. Any such paraphrases are so marked.

All images (except those for chs. 4, 7, and 8, which the author drew with Microsoft Shapes) are public domain vector images provided via download on publicdomainvectors.org and are bound to Creative Commons Deed CC0.

Dedicated to Bible re-readers everywhere

Psalm 19: His Art

The heavens declare the glory of God
And sunsets and rainbows are part of His art.
Where land touches water and sky touches sod
There hear I the voice of God in my heart.
The rocks and the plants and the animals talk,
Not human language, but deep in my heart.
They spoke, and my childish soul was awed
To feel the love that would power such art.

The beauty of the Word is bright, spelling love.
There are texture, shades, and surprise in the Word,
Similarities and parallelisms and a God who remembers.
There is rhythm in twos and in threes and in sevens,
Perspective and symmetry and a God who is fair.
There are turning points for a sudden "Aha!"
There are circles and closure and ending and peace,
There are lines of beauty in nature and Bible.

More to be followed are these than the pictures I paint,
Poems I pen, or careers I chase.
By them I meet the mind of God and acquaint
Soul of mine with a love I can face.
Long time ago the God who created this art
Made an agreement to carry me through.
Now, though the years and the tears and the fears seemed so hard,
Beauty assures me His promise is true.
Beauty is something you long to give when in love.
Beauty and longing are part of His heart.
So let the thoughts of my heart and the words of my mouth,
Also the acts of my hands—be His art!

—WILMA ZALABAK

Contents

List of Tables

List of Figures

Introduction

WHAT IS ART?

IN THIS BOOK, I intend to begin a rather in-depth exploration of art and beauty as I discover them in the Bible. My purpose is to draw your attention and readership to that book. In this endeavor, I will be showing you a way of reading that may seem alternative or additional to the way you have been accustomed to reading the Bible. This is not to denigrate or minimize the importance of the usual ways of reading. I merely beg you to add to your reading repertoire.

The first question that I face is this: What is art?

For this study I use the term *art* more as connoted from "artfulness" rather than from "artifact." An artifact is an item that, through observation, can yield information about the lifestyle of a being or a civilization past or present. An artifact could appear quite artless, with no pattern or meaning other than being an expression of a lifestyle. On the other hand, someone who uses "artfulness" is creative and careful about crafting an item for a specific purpose. In artfulness, there is pattern and expectation. When I claim to find art in the Bible, I mean that I find patterns that lead or build expectations and then also fulfill or satisfy those expectations. I find recognition of harmony, beauty, and other signs that cause me to think there was a creative and careful crafter of this finished product somewhere along the line.

The second question I face is this: What is beauty?

Ah, this then is the question that stumps me. I have no idea what beauty is for myself, let alone what it is for another person. Oh, I know that some art produces in me joy and satisfaction, and I call it beauty. I know also that some things I might call beauty can yield in me great sadness or disturbance. Since I observe apparently similar effects in other people, there must be something that, when seen or heard, affects some humans in ways that are common among those humans. As to whether this is a learned or shaped behavior, or described in other ways, I will leave the research to others more skilled. I will seek here to live within and describe what is, what I observe and feel. This is my witness here.

The third question I face is this: What is my purpose?

If I cannot, within the scope of this short book, plumb the depths of popular taste and perceptions of beauty, do I have any indication that anyone at all will read and resonate with what I find beautiful? Well, I am trusting that I have sensibilities in common with some, at least. I will share here what I call beauty in the Bible, what brings me joy or "Aha!" or sadness or "Oops!" If what I share speaks to you, I would love to hear from you.

Eugene Peterson, the translator of *The Message* version of the Bible, deftly describes my larger purpose. "Beauty is never only what our senses report to us but always also a sign of what is just beyond our senses—an innerness and depth. There is more to beauty than we can account for empirically. In that more and beyond we discern God."[1]

BEAUTY'S IDEAL

For me, the example, epitome, and ideal of beauty is in nature. By nature, I mean the things around us on this planet that humans did not make. Sure, one could argue that nature has much about it that is not beautiful. Yet I find so much in nature that is beautiful, and more beautiful than any human creation, that I will still take nature as my ideal of beauty in the work of this book.

---

1. Peterson, *Leap Over a Wall*, 85.

I want to show you beauty in the Bible, and I need some definition or example of beauty for comparison.

I thought about using any number of examples from other fields in order to illustrate my idea of beauty; however, I discovered that many of those fields take their essential ideas of beauty from nature. The fields of poetry, fiction, journalism, music, architecture, rhetoric, photography, painting, sculpture, drawing, painting, preaching, and many more exhibit fine examples of outstanding beauty. It was in comparing these fields, hunting for some common denominator underlying all their ideas of beauty, that I returned to nature in my quest.

After all, Jesus himself sent me to nature for surpassing ideas of beauty. He said, "Observe the flowers in the outdoors" (Matt 6:28 author paraphrase), and he compared their beauty to the splendor of the court and clothing of the most splendid king in all his hearers' history. Jesus said the flowers are beyond comparing to the most beautiful things this rich and wise king could create or import (Matt 6:26–30).

In these chapters on beauty and art in the Bible, let us cite the beauties of nature to find similar beauties in the Bible. I want to examine and discuss the sight elements of line, shape, color, movement, depth, and symmetry, and something further about sound, fragrance, and function.

The purpose of my quest, and now of my writing, is to show you why I love reading the Bible and to persuade you to try reading it purely for its enjoyment—you and God enjoying some beauty together—rather than with a heavy load of other reasons.

HOW BEAUTY CAPTIVATES

Since I have laid the groundwork to use my own experience about beauty, you will excuse me from citing surveys and electrodes and other sorts of empirical studies and their reports about various persons and their varied perceptions of beauty. Thank you.

Then what is it in beauty that most captivates me?

I can sometimes look at a color or other simplest element in the outdoors, and it comes over me that I could look at that thing forever. This is what I mean by being captivated; but this is not how I would describe the part that most captivates me.

Line, shape, movement, depth, symmetry—each of these can capture my delighted attention and cause me to call it beauty. This is what I mean by being captivated; but this is not the part that most captivates me.

Sometimes I have thought it is all these elements put together in an imaginative way that holds my attention and becomes beauty to me. Well, this, too, is what I mean by being captivated. Yet there is something else that most captivates me about beauty.

It has to do with patterns. Tony Hillerman wrote of old knowledge, "The only goal for man was beauty, and that beauty was found only in harmony, and that this harmony of nature was a matter of dazzling complexity. . . . In all things a pattern, and in this pattern, the beauty of harmony. . . . And thus one learned, gradually and methodically, if one was lucky, to always 'go in beauty,' to always look for the pattern, and to find it."[2] Yes, for me, there is a definite "Aha!" and "Eureka!" when I recognize a pattern, yet for me the captivating power of beauty has to do with more than discovering a pattern.

I am standing quite still in the middle of the stubbled hayfield, the evening mists rising and bringing to me the fragrances of the earth and the dried grasses. I hear a bobwhite call, two syllables. I wait and listen for the other call, as my brother had taught me to do. There it is, an answering call. I stand enraptured for a while expecting each return call according to the discovered pattern and noticing the variations on the pattern: sometimes a three-syllable call, sometimes two syllables; sometimes a long wait, sometimes the calls nearly at the same moment; the loci of the sources moving ever closer together in the evening air. I am captivated.

On another night, I am sitting on a stone next to a two-hour-old campfire. I watch the gold dancing among the many caverns created by the coals and half-burned wood. There are patterns in the flames, and there are variations on the patterns. A log shifts, and

2. Hillerman, *Dance Hall of Dead*, 76–77.

sparks shoot, and colors change, red, orange, yellow, gold, and some blues. I find my focus on a branch with about nine inches burning gently and segmented into pieces that look like grey marshmallows. One marshmallow drops off the end and glows on the golden floor. I expect the next marshmallow to fall, and I watch for it to do so. I am captivated.

For me, the magical captivating power of beauty lies in its ability to create expectations by its patterns, to heighten and lengthen my anticipation over time and throughout variations, and to satisfy the anticipation it created. The bobwhite did answer, and every time it did, I felt a little emotional boost, a joy in the satisfaction of the expectation. The next marshmallow did fall with a color show, and when it did, I felt a little turning in my soul, a tiny joy that I had stayed to see it satisfy my expectation.

Beauty in nature has a way of creating expectations and fulfilling them, while sometimes stringing out anticipation to rising heights of interest and emotion. Indeed, it uses delay, variations, and twists on the expectations to make patterns more difficult to spot and more rewarding to recognize. Yet, for me, the small fulfilling of the expectations it creates, and even the twists where it does not produce the expected event, call me back repeatedly to the thing I call beauty.

I think the Bible, by its very structure, creates expectations, draws out anticipations, and delivers delightful "Aha!" moments of fulfilling those expectations. Much of it is crafted with beauty in its structure, beauty of pattern, anticipation, and satisfactory recognitions. Though the promises of the Bible may take centuries and even millennia to reach fulfillment, I can right now read the Bible and find fulfillment of my most poignant anticipations. Sometimes, in the stretching out of the longing, I experience a kind of haunting joy in the anticipation. I believe much of this anticipation and fulfillment seeps in subliminally for most people, without awareness to the conscious mind. In my next few chapters, I want to raise some awareness of this beauty.

This anticipation-fulfillment power of beauty is the reason I sometimes feel with joy "Here is a book that understands me!"

JESUS CITED ANTICIPATIONS IN NATURE

In the previous section, I observed that what I call beauty has much to do with the way something arouses my expectations and then fulfills them or does not. I believe Jesus cited the same phenomenon, the captivating power of anticipation.

Jesus told the story of a man who planted grain all over his field, and while he slept an enemy came and planted weeds in the same field. When the servants and master viewed what grew, it was not what they had expected. Hereby Jesus introduced tension into the story, the tension between anticipation and not-fulfillment. The rest of the story builds that anticipation, asking and answering "How did this happen?" and "What shall we do about it?" The conclusion of the story asks the hearers to stay in anticipation until the resolution at the time of harvest. Read it for yourself in Matt 13:24–30, 36–43.

LITERATURE REVIEW

This is not a book on the theology of beauty, the love of God for beauty, or even any of the Bible's uses of or settings for the word "beauty." This is not a book to define and describe the Bible's acrostics, parallelisms, chiasms, parables, and other figures of speech, though these could be called art. This book consists of the notes of an artist enjoying a gallery. I study what something beautiful means in my heart, why an artist might use this or that piece of beauty, and what effect the beautiful might have on my inner soul.

I have been helped along in this gallery by one of my favorite preaching professors, Fred Craddock. Craddock wrote, "So predominant have become the concerns for facticity and historicity that any aesthetic appreciation of the Bible is immediately regarded as a device for avoiding the subject matter."[3] I have made the same observation and therefore acquiesce to a truly short literature review here.

3. Craddock, *Overhearing the Gospel*, 57.

Robert Alter was the first one I noticed who seemed to be reaching for my niche. Alter wrote, "The literary vehicle is so much the necessary medium through which the Hebrew writers realized their meanings that we will grasp the meanings at best imperfectly if we ignore their fine articulations as literature."[4] The Hebrew writers, including those of both Testaments, used fine art to create meaning and to bring that meaning into the heart. Though I stand back from claiming to understand their full meanings, I crave connections with people who know such artistic meanings are present.

Perhaps this is why Fred Craddock could write, "It takes an artist to treat properly the artistry of a prophetic oracle."[5] Sit with me for a minute on this, please. Did not God make us all artists? Did not God fill us with creative gifts? Then let us let our artists out of their propositional-certainty cages to have a playdate together in the word of God!

Leonard Bernstein helped me in this. He wrote, "There is so much more joy and exaltation and spiritual food to be gotten out of that Brahms First than you get by simply enjoying the tunes, the mellow sound of the strings, the lyrical improvisations of the woodwinds, or the majestic utterances of the brass. There is the structure . . . , the structure. The harmonic flow, the architectural build—."[6] I feel the frustration Bernstein must have felt trying to get people to hear and talk about the structure and flow that made his passions soar.

I deeply longed for acquaintances and conversations that could help me open myself to increasing helpings of the beauty in the Bible, by helping me understand what was happening. Robert Jourdain moved into that arena with this comment: "Music sets up anticipations and then satisfies them. It can withhold its resolutions, and heighten anticipation by doing so, then to satisfy the anticipation in a great gush of resolution."[7] The great gush of resolution is for me like the pleasure of a scratch to an itch, or a stretch to a

---

4. Alter, *World of Biblical Literature*, 63–64.

5. Craddock, *Overhearing the Gospel*, 57.

6. Bernstein, *Infinite Variety of Music*, 21.

7. Jourdain, *Music, Brain, and Ecstasy*, 312.

cramped foot gone bare in the grass. I want to understand and share why the Bible is this to me.

Then I sat under Bernard Brandon Scott who taught the use of technology in preaching by showing his extraordinarily well-composed photos of incredibly beautiful scenes. I learned how to use technology, yet the greatest thing I took away was the art of what he did and his use of beauty. This is also where I gained my favorite book so far on beauty. Scott and his wife Margaret Lee wrote *Sound Mapping the New Testament*. Here are some excerpts put in order for you to follow the train of thought. Lee and Scott wrote:

> Recurrence of concepts and ideas as signified by various words engages silent readers in the construction of a written composition and thus increases reading satisfaction and enriches the quest for meaning.[8]

> Repetition serves as sound's most basic structuring device.[9]

> Repeated sounds draw attention. A repeated set of auditory signals recalls their previous articulation and invites an audience to reinterpret current sounds in light of sounds that have already occurred. Sounds are remembered in terms of the contributions they make to the emerging aesthetic whole.[10]

> As remembered patterns accumulate in memory, they acquire structure and build expectations for future sounds. A composition's sounds train the ear, both to attend to particular rhythms, patterns, and topics as the composition progresses and to retain them in memory.[11]

In other words, where I find repetition in the Bible, I might also find some organization or structure that would cause me to expect or anticipate some other repetition in some way. The very

---

8. Lee and Scott, *Sound Mapping*, 135.

9. Lee and Scott, *Sound Mapping*, 141.

10. Lee and Scott, *Sound Mapping*, 142.

11. Lee and Scott, *Sound Mapping*, 142.

act of recognizing that structure contributes to reader "satisfaction and enriches the quest for meaning."[12]

Add to that benefit the satisfaction of the "anticipation in a great gush of resolution,"[13] as Jourdain described it, and there seems to be a mountain of satisfaction possible to us while reading the Bible. To find something exactly where I was led to believe it would be produces a "Eureka!" moment for me. It is my proposal that there are many such moments available for us with God in the reading of the Bible.

I wonder if people in the nineteenth century, still in the Romantic period of music, perhaps read with more awareness of art and beauty. A favorite author of mine from that era, Ellen White, wrote, "The mind will enlarge if it is employed in tracing out the relation of the subjects of the Bible, comparing scripture with scripture, and spiritual things with spiritual. There is nothing more calculated to strengthen the intellect that the study of the Scriptures. No other book is so potent to elevate the thought, to give vigor to the faculties, as the broad, ennobling truths of the Bible."[14]

Eugene Peterson added, "Beauty releases light into our awareness so that we're conscious of the beauty of the Lord."[15]

Reader, if your awareness and consciousness of the beauty of the Lord increase while reading this little book, my work will have been worthwhile.

12. Lee and Scott, *Sound Mapping*, 135.
13. Jourdain, *Music, Brain, and Ecstasy*, 312.
14. White, *Steps to Christ*, 90.
15. Peterson, *Leap Over a Wall*, 86.

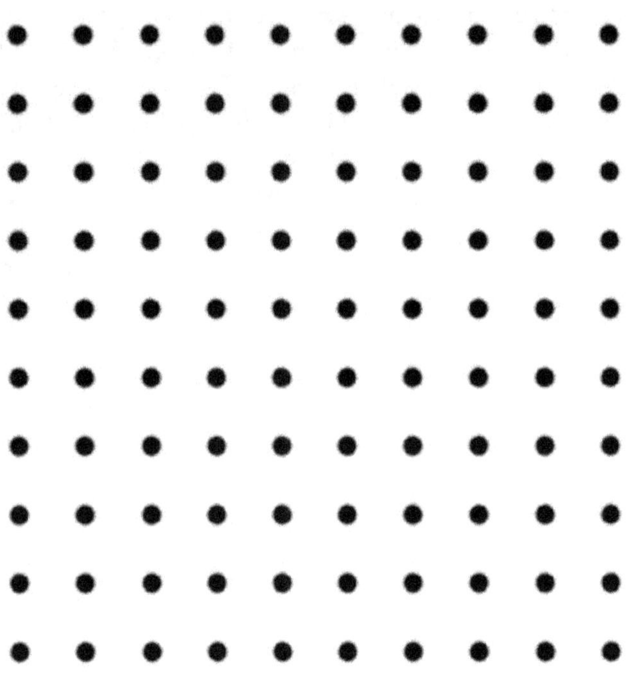

1

Points and Dots

It is probably too big for me, this project I have set for myself, to examine and discuss the sight elements of line, shape, color, movement, depth, and symmetry, and something further about sound, fragrance, and function. Further, I know that my purpose is too big for me. I wrote earlier, "The purpose for my quest, and now of my writing, is to show you why I love reading the Bible and to persuade you to try reading it purely for its enjoyment—you and God enjoying some beauty together—rather than with a heavy load of other reasons."

I have given my disclaimers. I recognize that beauty is so subjective, always "in the eye of the beholder," that I am choosing to tell this in first person rather than trying to cite all the many research studies and experiments on what people find or label beautiful. I have also explained that I will take nature as my ideal for beauty.

The first element of natural beauty on that preliminary list is "line." In geometry class I learned that a line starts with a point. That I why this first chapter is about points and dots in nature and in the Bible.

I am standing on a railroad tie in Nebraska looking west into the sunset. On and on the rails run like two strings of molten fire in the golden light. I know they run on and on, yet in my eyes they run only to a vanishing point on the horizon. A point. I expect that point though I cannot see it, and the expectation glues my attention to the scene.

I am eating breakfast in my tiny kitchen in Mississippi springtime. I hear one chirp and immediately turn my face to the window to catch the glimpse of red feathers and topknot that I had learned to expect with that chirp. Actually, I am wondering if it is the pet cardinal we rescued and raised last year and named Carl. One staccato chirp, crisply articulated and let go, holds all that meaning and beauty for me.

I think there are a couple of points like this in the Bible story, crisply articulated, expected, captivating. One such point would be the moment of the death of Jesus on the cross. Another such point for me would be the time humans chose to think that God might not be good after all, the beginning of sin. Both Jesus's death and Eve's bite took up only points in long time like the staccato cardinal's chirp, and both created and satisfied the expectations of millennia like the vanishing point on the railroad tracks. The beauty and mystery of these two points in time can keep me thinking and keep satisfying my soul's thirst for beauty, for a long time.

I have in my hand lots of dots of sand glued to strong paper. I touch but do not rub or scratch the sandpaper; it is a texture I do not find particularly pleasing. I use the sandpaper to make my desk beautiful. If I had lots and lots of dots of sand, I would have a desert or a seashore, and I would be captivated by the texture created by the dunes and the valleys. I would call it beauty.

I think of all the other stories between the points done by Eve and Jesus as texture to the big picture. Some are high points of determined trust in God, and some are low points of suspicion against God. Texture. It keeps me enthralled.

In one of those stories, God encouraged Abraham by mentioning that his descendants would be numberless as the sand of the seashore (Gen 22:17). I believe God used the picture of sand because its dots and texture would seem beautiful and bathe with beauty the thinking of Abraham and of us.

Points and dots and texture. Can you find more illustrations of these elements of beauty in the Bible? Will you decide to read the Bible for the beauty God put there to feed your soul? Yes, that is good.

2

Straight Lines

I AM SNUGGLING WITH my Chihuahua dog, Skippy, in the living room of our three-story, square farmhouse in central Wisconsin, the house where I grew up. The sofa cover is slick vinyl and cold except where I sit with Skippy on my lap. His hair is short and straight, and I am watching how each hair interacts with each other along his tail as he wags it. The smooth texture along his back calls for the sweep of my hand, over and over and over. The soft smooth texture on the side of his nose invites my kiss.

Straight lines can create texture.

I waken and crawl out of my sleeping bag in the mountains of Colorado. In just a few minutes, the sun will crest the lower mountains across from me. The lodgepole pines in my canyon forest draw my eyes upward. Their trunks stand tall and straight, parallel arrows pointing to the sky. Even their needles are long and straight, making a thatchwork texture of fallen needles on the ground where I sit. I watch the evidence of the sunrise sweeping down the slope above me, and then it flows over me like a caress. The sunlight spreads all around me. And in the slight mist of the early morning, I can see the slanting rays of light reaching the forest floor. Perhaps there is nothing so enchanting to me as golden beams of light slanting between tall pine trees. Though I cannot touch it, I crave to bathe in it.

Straight lines, whether parallel or crosshatch, create texture. They draw the eye. They create in me an anticipation about what it must feel like.

Let us talk a bit first about texture in the Bible. I like to read a variety of translations of the Bible because each one has a different texture. Some march right along like straight lines, while others meander a bit more. Furthermore, within one translation there is a variety of texture. Psalms and Proverbs often state a straightforward thesis and then lay down a parallel thesis next to it, or sometimes the second thesis does not lie exactly parallel but takes off straight on in a different direction. On the other hand, the Letter to the Philippians does some meandering while often returning to the theme of giving thanks. Each genre of the Bible has a different feel or texture: poetry, letter, prophecy, story. It is fun to notice such things.

It is great to notice, but what if I do not notice? I think this art of the Bible has its subliminal effect whether or not I notice the structure. I believe God put it together in ways to accomplish what he designed to accomplish whether or not I understand the mechanisms of this accomplishment. Indeed, I am sure I have no idea of the full efficacy of what God has put in his word. This is merely a tip-of-the-iceberg kind of introduction to some little-considered reasons to read the Bible.

And what does texture in the Bible do for me? It draws me in. Whichever texture I am dealing with at the moment calls me to interact in some way. Maybe it invites another touch. Maybe it draws my eyes upward. Maybe it makes me crave to bathe in it.

Straight lines can create texture. In the Bible straight lines can create anticipation and, through that anticipation and its satisfaction, grant me some of the most exquisite pleasure and joy of which this human is capable.

3

Curved Lines

I AM SITTING AT my desk in middle school in Wisconsin. The posterboard is too big for my desktop, but I am making do. The material is almost matte enough to take the color well from my colored pencils. I am making a poster for the health poster contest. On my poster there are rolling hills, a small lake, a curving road, a few trees, and on the lake, two swans conversing. Their conversation takes up several lines in a bubble beside each beautifully curving neck. The bubble is about two inches wide and deep. The topic of the conversation is a warning not to destroy the beauty of the place. I worked hard on that poster. I took great care to make the curves exquisite and the shade transitions smooth. I made it a thing of beauty in my eyes.

Oh, and I did not win the contest! One adult came to me afterward, with great commendation for the obvious artistry of thought and production that went into that poster. She explained that it just did not fit the category of poster where the message must be large and bold. With that, I thought some more about the various forms of art. I always thought.

I am driving north in Georgia into the Blue Ridge, the southern tip of the Smoky Mountains. I can hardly drive for the continual pulling of my eyes to study the shades and varieties of green in the canopy of trees. The canopy is dressed in a variety of distinct shades of spring green. Might I know the tree by the shade of green? This is not likely, because that shade will change again by this afternoon. Find the one that is most yellow. Which is redder? That one has a silver sheen. I wish I could set them in order of shade, yet each tree-top holds infinite variety within itself. These and any many other ideas are born in my mind and soul by each glimpse of beauty I steal on my way driving north in Georgia. I reach my destination strangely stilled and filled with joy and strength.

Curved lines suggest to me the ideas of gradation and serenity. They set anticipations alive in me, anticipations of peaceful movement and arrival at a satisfying whole in time. They build patience to keep the serenity until the whole thing makes sense.

The Bible is full of curved lines in the form of gradual unveilings and step by step gradations. Let me illustrate.

- In Ps 1:1, there is a progression of three: walk, stand, sit.

- The psalmist wrote Ps 119 as an acrostic with each set of eight verses containing eight sayings that begin with the same letter of the Hebrew alphabet, and with consecutive sets of eight using each of the letters of the Hebrew alphabet in order.

- Daniel's king had a future-telling dream in which consecutively listed metals are progressively both less valuable and more durable, in Dan 2.

- Jesus used progression when he said, "Ask, seek, knock," as recorded in Matt 7:7.

- Peter wrote the ladder that begins "Add to your faith virtue, . . ." in 2 Pet 1:5–7.

- The book of Revelation delights in progressions of sevens; for instance, see Rev 2–3.

These are only a few of the many, many instances of gradation and progression in the Bible. Their very gradualness captures my attention and fills me with patience in waiting for the denouement, and with joy in anticipating. I believe the Bible is written as art in such a way as to use its structure to help produce in the reader the very attributes of which it speaks. This can be done either subliminally or consciously. Perhaps the work can be enhanced if I also express gratitude for the artistic structure of this Bible—as I read it.

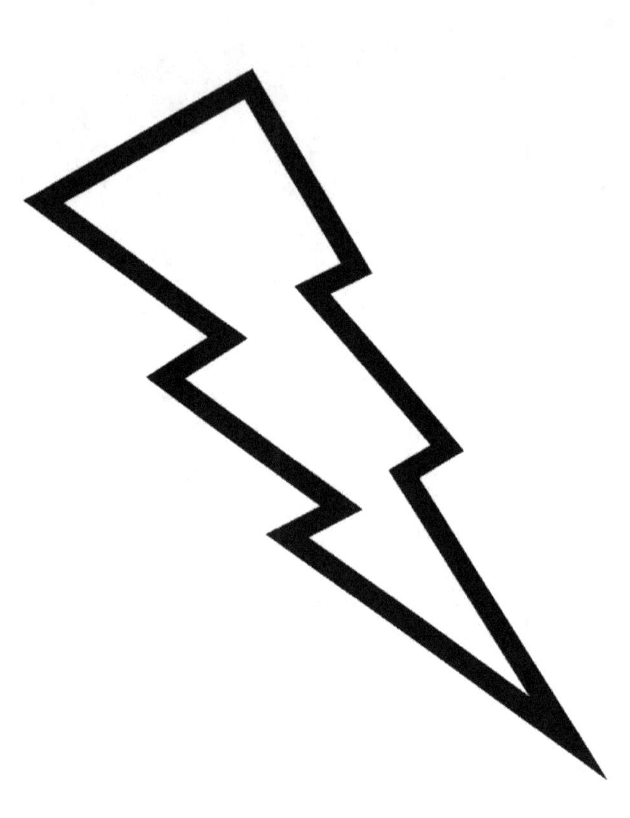

4

Jagged Lines

I AM CAMPING SOMEWHERE in the mountains of Colorado. I have been awakened by the rain on my tent, and I lie there listening. The constant pitter-patter and the warmth inside the sleeping bag lull me almost back to sleep. There have been some thunder rumbles and lightning flashes but nothing that would not just keep on lulling me to sleep. Then—boom clap! and a huge bright light envelopes my tent. The light dissipates, and the clap rolls way. More thunder and lightning enliven the night, and by then I am ready for them, even peeking out a bit to watch. Perhaps because it can surprise me so thoroughly, I usually think of lightning as jagged lines through the sky.

Next morning, I dry out my gear in the sunlight while listening to the canyon wren's song. This song begins high in pitch and descends the scale. I do not know if it is the same scale as in Western music, and that is okay. The song descends step by step, and one might think it will go on forever. Then, surprise, there is a note out of order. It sounds like several notes together in a great big "Whee!" My anticipation is built up by the continually descending notes, then the finale does not give me what I expected. Yet now, after hearing this song many times, I have come to anticipate the surprise ending, and I have great glee in hearing it no matter how many times. I would call the canyon wren's song a jagged line.

I am taking my daily walk in the woods near my home in Georgia. There is that strange tree with two tops. Apparently the one top was broken off long ago, and two side branches took over the function of the top. Side by side they stand as if twins doing double duty for the fallen parent, their footing creating a jagged line compared to the first tree trunk. The philodendron in my kitchen had an accident that killed the budding end. A new bud came out at a strange angle below the injury and grew to be the main plant. Still there is a jagged line where it came out of the first stem.

Jagged lines surprise the expectations previously built. Beautiful jagged lines bring satisfaction of expectation even within the surprise. Humans enjoy jagged lines.

For further illustration of human enjoyment of jagged lines let me draw a bit from common social conversation. A joke with three wrong answers builds expectation, and then the punch line satisfies expectation but not the expectation built by the previous answers. Wordplay builds expectations simply through the common use of the word, and then overturns those expectations by switching to another meaning of that word, which actually satisfies another set of expectations much better than those in the anticipation. Irony builds expectations on two different levels at the same time: the expectations of the character in the story as he or she moves through the events, and the expectations of the reader who knows so much more than the character knows. The release and satisfaction come when both expectations get resolved, with learning for both.

Jagged lines abound in the Bible.

Take Exod 3, where Moses herds sheep according to expectation. He sees an unexpected fire. He turns aside in an unexpected fashion. He expects the landscape, at least the tree, to be damaged by the fire. His expectation is turned on its head when God himself speaks to Moses out of the burning bush. There is no damage, only an unexpected call from God.

Take Num 22, where the reader knows an angel is standing in Balaam's way and that Balaam's donkey sees the angel, but Balaam does not. The reader feels with Balaam during all three beatings he gives his donkey for not taking him straight on the path. The reader also feels with the donkey being beaten unfairly for something he could not help. In this way the anticipation builds in the reader. And then, surprise! The donkey talks! Never saw that coming! But now when I read the story, I surely look for it over and over again.

Take Luke 20:22–37 (author paraphrase), where Jesus answers a question with a nonanswer, twice. First question: "Should we pay taxes?" Nonanswer: "Whose picture is on the money?" and "Give whatever to whomever it belongs." Second question: "Which wife gets the husband in heaven?" Nonanswer: "You don't know what you're talking about" (see also Matt 22:29) and "Let me tell you there is life after death." The reader expects an answer, and there is no answer.

Yet perhaps that unmet expectation will call the reader to consider the context in Luke 20:2–8 (author paraphrase). Question: "Who authorized you?" Nonanswer: "Tell me first who authorized John the Baptist?" (But the men, being politicians, were stumped over popular opinion on that question.) "We can't answer," they said. Nonanswer: "Neither will I answer you." Now, perhaps we can anticipate that Jesus will not answer some questions put to him.

Take Rev 13, where an animal appears looking like a lamb. The reader has certain expectations of a lamb, silence sometimes, pitiful bleat at other times. But, surprise! This lamb speaks like a dragon!

It is all about anticipation. Jagged lines do not meet expectations in the ways expected. Jagged lines do not satisfy anticipations in the ways anticipated. However, there is grand satisfaction, which keeps a person enthralled, captivated until the final line. I believe reading the Bible can keep me enthralled through all the surprises of life until the final line. And then, I believe, I will be satisfied, yet probably not in the way I expected.

Next time, parallel lines. One of these times I will take a breather here to discuss some hindrances and objections I have run into about this way of reading the Bible, for the beauty of it.

5

Parallel Lines

I AM COMING BACK to the house from the woods where I gathered spring flowers in Wisconsin. Since the cow path I am following is a little too narrow for my natural gait, I have to concern myself with staying balanced while putting one foot directly in front of the other. Well, I would not have to be so careful except that the hooves of the cows have dug this path about four inches deep compared to the pasture around it. I could walk with one foot on the grass and one in the path, but the four-inch difference requires as much thought to navigate as does the narrowness of the path. I could walk with both feet in the grass, but of course the cows use the shortest path and avoid rocks, trees, and most puddles. I walk the cow path and learn to keep my balance. At some time in my youth or childhood, I notice that the two sides of this cow path are amazingly parallel. The beauty of a cow path for me lies in letting its parallel lines lead my imagination on, on into the barn where it is warm, on under the trees of the woods, on wherever the cow path goes.

My brother and I are playing hide-and-seek among the tall green stalks in our cornfield. The pennant-like leaves whip us and grab at us. The new-corn fragrance seeps into our hair, our clothes, and our breathing chambers for remembering later. I lie down in the valley between two rows. The stalks above me stand straight and parallel. My eyes follow their parallel lines, and soon my imagination is captivated in the sweep of going on and on through the infinity of space.

I am captivated by the wonders of sound. No natural sound reaches my ears with only one frequency. The sound finds complementary vibrations wherever it goes. The string or the air will vibrate at one frequency, and at another frequency exactly half the first, and at another exactly half that, and on and on. If strong enough, it will touch any other string or chamber in tune with it and set that to vibrating too. In this way, any natural sound carries with it parallel sounds and we call it beauty.

Parallel lines hold my attention and bring me pleasure. Discovering how one line follows the other, or does not, excites my interest. I can spend days thinking of similarities and contrasts, especially in the Bible.

Take Ps 19:7–9, for instance. The pattern sets up immediately, and then continues through four more similar revolutions about the wonders of the word of God. "The [noun] of the Lord is [adjective], [adverbial '-ing' phrase]." The sixth revolution extends the adjective and discards the adverbial phrase. A structure that produces parallel lines is a highly effective construction to keep me enthralled, wondering where else this word of God might lead me.

Take 1 Cor 13:4–7, for another instance. The pattern "Love [is or is not, does or does not do]" goes through fifteen parallel thoughts, a beautiful passage for any orator to present. Perhaps the ways of extolling love, or maybe love itself, could go on and on and on as pictured in the parallel lines.

To take this idea to another level, you will enjoy noticing that the "Hymn to Love" in 1 Cor 13, in its well-planned, three-sectioned structure, is parallel to the "Hymn to God" in Ps 19. I think the later author, Paul writing to the Corinthians, could have intentionally copied the structure of the earlier psalm.

In the book of Revelation, one thing people often notice first is the groupings of seven. Several of those sevens carry words and phrases that appear to make them parallel with others of those sevens. This thought brings me back to the little schoolhouse in Wisconsin where I sat making charts of those sevens, admiring the similarities and differences I discovered.

There is more, and this has captured my admiring attention for years by now. I found that Revelation follows Daniel like one line follows another in parallel construction. This is how I came upon it. I noticed first that Rev 13 holds a striking number of words and images similar to those of Dan 7. Next, I noticed that each of these passages lies pretty close to the physical center of its book. I counted pages and verses to find the proportions before and after these chapters in their respective books nearly identical. That led me to look for other parallels. First, I used common interpretations to see if the topics were the same. Then I realized humans can put a title on any passage to make it look like it matches another. I needed a more objective study method. That is when I learned Greek and Hebrew and lined up similar words and images, depending only on those of three or more matching words in sequence. I do believe that these parallel lines, like the rails of a railroad, invite me to look on beyond into an eternity with God.

Daniel	Revelation
1:12, 14 Prove, ten days	2:10 Be tried, ten days
2:29, 45 Come to pass hereafter	1:19; 4:1 Be hereafter
3:25 I see four, in the midst	5:6 I beheld four, in the midst
4:34 Honored him that liveth forever	4:9 Glory, him who liveth forever
5:23 Silver, gold, brass, wood, stone, see not, nor hear	9:20 Gold, silver, brass, stone, wood, neither see, nor hear
7:3–21 Great beasts came up from the sea, a lion, a bear, a leopard, ten horns, a mouth speaking great things, made war with the saints	13:1–7 A beast rises up out of the sea, ten horns, a leopard, a bear, a lion, a mouth speaking great things, make war with the saints
7:25; 12:7 A time and times and the dividing of time	12:14 A time, and times, and half a time
8:10 Of heaven, the stars to the ground	12:4 The stars of heaven, to the earth
12:4, 9 The words, seal the book, time	22:7–10 Seal not the sayings, book, time

Table 01. Daniel and Revelation: Three Matching Words in Sequence[1]

1. Though there are many more matching words and scenes in this case, I chose to list only those that show at least three Greek words in order. See Aland et al., *Greek New Testament*, 836–95; Brenton, *Septuagint*, 1049–70.

I have been captivated for many years by the beauty of the parallel lines in God's word. I have read these parallels over and over and over, thrilling with the similarities and differences they manifest and the eternity to which they lead.

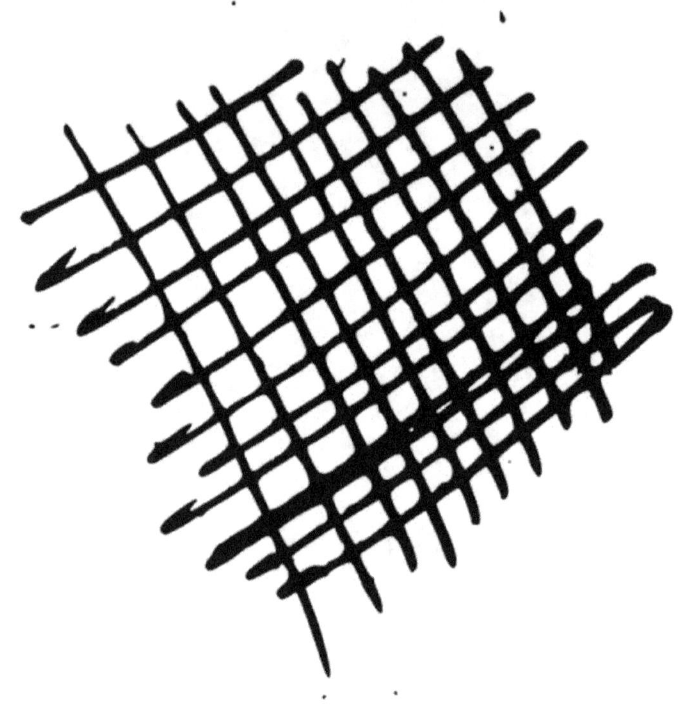

6

Transverse Lines

I AM SITTING ON a slope beside the mountain road in Colorado. I know soon I will hear the sound of trotting hooves as my friend rides her horse home. I know this will be a trot because this horse is spoiled and, though her feet slowly plod away from home, the minute her face is turned toward home she breaks into a trot and maintains that gait around all curves until she gains the hitching post. Here they come. The sound gets louder. My friend's screams, as they make a hairpin turn, almost separating in their progress, strike my ears along with the steady hoofbeats. The sound gets louder as they approach, the hoofbeats rhythmically marking and intensifying the straight line of the sound. I remember how I love the sound of approaching horse's hoofbeats. I love it so much I learned to drum my fingers in somewhat of a mimic of the sound of a horse's trot.

I will try to describe here what is beauty to me in transverse lines. In this usage, transverse means something that might look like a number sign or a pound sign or a sharp sign in music, or a tic-tac-toe game starter. For our purposes today, transverse lines will be two or more lines that cross, at the same angle, another one or more lines.

I am looking west in wintertime across the snow and rolling farmlands in central Wisconsin. The sun is setting behind the hills.

The trees on the hill horizon stand starkly silhouetted against the colors of the sky at sunset. The trees create transverse lines to the one line of the horizon. I could ponder it forever, but the colors fade, the light dims, and I must go home to study.

I am sitting at the dining room table in our big farmhouse in Wisconsin. My mother holds a ball for the sun and a marble for the earth (for a science lesson) in her hands. This is the first time I have understood how the days and years are made. It hits me like a new day, granting me a huge "Aha!" Somehow, I get the months figured out too. In the line of a year, the days or months become the transverse lines. In the line of a month, or in the parallel lines of two months, the days are the transverse lines.

Transverse lines call me to think creatively, to organize my categories of thought in new ways. They give me rhythm, and sometimes they change my rhythms.

I remember the first time I saw a calendar flipped to number the days down the page rather than across the page. The line of the ongoing month went down instead of across, and the transverse lines of the days cut the line of the month at regular intervals, marching down rather than across. Transverse lines provide rhythm and much more. They provide a rubric for creating a new paradigm. All I have to do is switch the axes, the "across" and "down" elements, and I have an entirely new way to view the subject. Transverse lines invite me to think creatively.

I was in a meeting the other day where a roomful of people finally understood each other just because someone stood up and flipped the axes in the chart on the board. What a tool switching the axes might be!

I will describe two instances in the Bible where transverse lines have enthralled me for hundreds of hours and continue to thrill me.

Matthew wrote things twice. There are many cases in which he placed the exact same verbiage in two different settings.

Compare		
Matt 1:16	Matt 27:17	Jesus who is called Christ
Matt 2:2	Matt 27:37	King of the Jews
Matt 3:17	Matt 17:5	beloved Son . . . well pleased
Matt 6:15	Matt 18:35	Father in heaven . . . forgive
Matt 7:12	Matt 22:35–40	the law and the prophets
Matt 7:20	Matt 12:33	known by your fruit
Matt 7:22–23	Matt 25:11–12, 41	I never knew you . . . depart
Matt 8:23–24	Matt 14:30–31	Lord, save us . . . faith
Matt 9:13	Matt 12:7	mercy and not sacrifice
Matt 10:39	Matt 16:25	find life . . . lose life . . .
Matt 12:29	Matt 16:4	sign of Jonah
Matt 13:12	Matt 25:29	will be given more
Matt 19:30	Matt 20:16	first last . . . last first
Matt 24:30	Matt 26:64	coming in the clouds

Table 02. Twice in Matthew[1]

These doubles in Matthew seem to create dozens of attention-getting stops along the ongoing line of Matthew's story. I think of them as transverse lines, and yes, I have tried all sorts of ways to organize them and switch the axes on them, and I have not yet found the reason or pattern that will thrill me. I think it is out there for someone to find!

The book of Revelation, as many readers notice, presents several groups of seven, some more obviously parallel to each other than others, by their words and phrases. I made charts and more charts of the sevens, usually with the title and reference citation along the horizontal axis and the seven steps, or stages, along the vertical axis. I found more sevens and some in Daniel with interesting verbal parallels to each other.

Now, please, in your mind's eye switch the axes. Make the seven steps, or stages, go horizontally. Does it give you a new viewpoint? For me, I saw the sevens as transverse lines providing rhythm and expansion to the story line or plot. This method of seeing invited

---

1. This is merely a sampling among many.

me to play with switching the axes on other charts, to consider seeing the world and the word in new ways, to think creatively.

I have been at this for a while now and see no letting up. I am
drawn forever by beauty in the Bible.

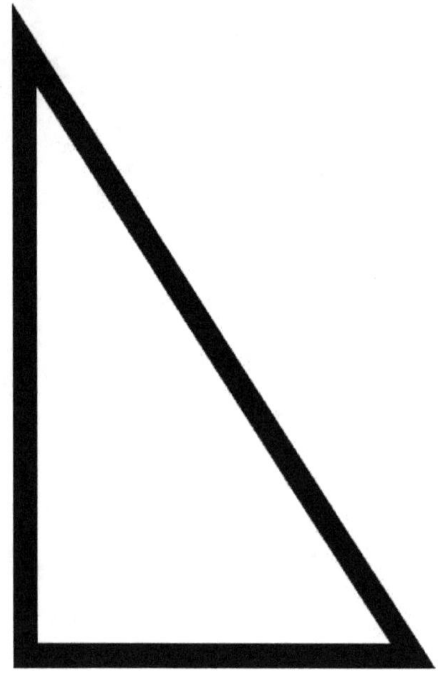

7

Angle Lines

THE FENCE POSTS HAVE white caps. The car snuggles under a white blanket. It has been a quiet winter night in Wisconsin. The sunlight breaks over a quiet world. I cannot take my eyes from studying the fence posts with their white caps. Every cap is especially shaped and suited for its fence post. Some posts are round, some are triangular, some slant, some are fallen. Every post has a cap to suit. Every cap is perfectly symmetrical with its post.

I am noticing trees as my mother and I drive through the summertime in Wisconsin. I remember doing this in the wintertime also, with the trees shorn of leaves and each proudly displaying the symmetry God gave to that individual. Every tree has its own symmetry that is captivatingly beautiful. If it stands alone in the field, it seems filled out quite symmetrically. If it stands among other trees, its symmetry complements that of those around it. If it stands against a building or mountain, still it strikes me with its symmetry in its own setting. For a while I believed symmetry was the primary element of beauty.

This leads me to think in terms of angle lines, a point at the top with the lines diverging toward the bottom. That does work even for dogwoods and bonsai, as I learned in flower arranging class. The diverging lines do not have to be totally delineated for the arrangement to look symmetrical and beautiful. All that is needed is the point and two strong suggestions of diverging lines, one such suggestion on each side and one farther down than the other.

It was some time before I learned that the sunlight itself by God's design created the symmetry in the trees, drawing their branches and leaves to available light. Therefore, a tree struck by lightning or otherwise mutilated will in a few years look beautiful again with a new symmetry.

On my first night's camping in Colorado, I am listening to the nighthawk's call. It has taken me several days to perceive that the call I hear comes from those incessantly darting birds. I think the nighthawks' wings in flight create such ever-changing angles and symmetry that I could watch them forever. They swoop close to me and utter that screech. Well, I guess I can hear the screech in angle terms also, with a point in the middle where it turns back on itself and fades away. I am getting used to the sound as just another part of this beautiful dusk in the mountains.

Since symmetry may have been one of my first observations of beauty in nature, I also find great joy in discovering symmetry in the Bible. Jokes and proverbs and parables all have in common the idea of symmetry. Symmetry helps their pacing to get the listeners ready, with intense anticipation, for the punch line. Some have two elements in antithesis (see Ps 1; Prov 16:8–9; Matt 24:44–51). Some have three elements in strong interrelation (see Prov 30:15–31; Matt 25:14–30).

I will cite here four instances of this angle line structure, this symmetry, in the Bible.

For number 1, please look at Ps 19. There are three sections to this ancient hymn: God revealed in nature (Ps 19:1–6), God revealed in his word (Ps 19:7–10), and God revealed in humans (Ps 19:11–14). I can view any of those sections as the top point and then see the other two as defining the angle. It makes a beautiful picture whichever piece I put at the top, the picture of God revealing Godself.

The sectioning is revealed by changes in rhythm and texture. I notice the transverse lines and how they are different lengths in one section compared to another. I notice the texture created by the words and images, different in each section. By changes in rhythm and texture, I can identify the various sections of a hymn or poem.

For number 2, now look at 1 Cor 13. I find three sections in this ancient poem: Love's preeminence (1 Cor 13:1–3), Love's description (1 Cor 13:4–8), Love's fruit and future (1 Cor 13:9–13). If I see Love's preeminence as the top point, I can see description on one side and fruit and future on the other side, creating a beautiful symmetrical picture of love. It draws me not only into the picture to study it and remember it, but also into thinking in the ways of love.

As number 3, I pray the Lord's Prayer. Some call it the Our Father. It is recorded in Matt 6:9–13 and has been translated and sung in many languages and many keys. The first section is adoration to God. The second section is human requests. The third section returns to the adoration of God in a new way. I think one of the reasons this prayer is so beloved all around the world is its beauty, its symmetry, its simple angle lines in such a small space.

For number 4, look at Rev 14:6–12 and find three angels mentioned. I will summarize the message of each like this: 1) worship God (Rev 14:6–7); 2) false worship is ruined (Rev 14:8); 3) choose today whom to worship (Rev 14:9–12). For me, this set of three is fuller and more glorious than many others. It has captured my heart for weeks on end. Their theme and the big picture has connections with, and gives new meaning to, many other threes in the Bible. I will continue, maybe through eternity, to read Revelation for the beauty in it.

I tried to show you my joy in angle lines and in the beauty they yield in nature and the Bible. This is why I return day after day to the reading of the Bible.

8

Arrow Lines

ARROW LINES, FOR OUR purposes here, are two opposite angle lines lying in close proximity.

I am overlooking a lake in the early morning light and stillness in Colorado. The aspens are turning golden, their leaves reflecting richly with not a breath to stir them. The trees' uprightness, as well as the curve of the skyline at their tops, create angle lines with the shore of the lake that lies opposite me. As the new sunlight nudges itself over my shoulder to face the scene, I watch the image of the trees grow downward on the glassy surface of the lake. The image below is mirror to the image above, the angle lines exquisitely opposite, creating arrow lines pointing left and right. I wish I could capture this moment forever. I cannot. Instead, I find myself gazing long at the next nature photograph calendar I find that features mirror images. The beauty of it captivates me.

I think I have never found an intersection of two opposites in nature that did not enthrall me. Dawn and dusk posit light and dark, day and night, close together. A storm and its rainbow require warm air and cold air close, clouds and sunlight mixing. Shore brings land and water together; horizon brings earth and sky together. Fall and spring make the more extreme seasons kiss each other. The Sabbath commandment includes both work and rest.

These and many more such opposites drawn together entice me into their worlds of beauty.

Here I introduce the technical word *chiasm*. The word comes from the Greek alphabet letter *chi*, which looks like an *x*. The letter *x* is a mirror image, the bottom half matching in reverse order the top half. There are several images one could use to picture this. Sometimes it is called the "envelope" construction, the things in the middle enveloped between two "bookends." I sometimes use the image of nesting dolls, because I can take the big doll apart and find another inside it, which I can take apart to find yet another, the smaller dolls each being enclosed between two halves of the next larger doll. In this chapter, I liken chiasm to arrow lines in art, two opposing angle lines in close proximity.

Apparently Hebrew and Jewish children learned the alphabet backward as well as forward, and often told their stories in the memorable form of revisiting in reverse order all the items mentioned in the first half of the story. Not only does this form provide an effective mnemonic device, but it also shapes the impact of the story. This time I want to discuss the intersection of the opposites, the point at which the story turns, the "Aha!" moment, the proximity of opposites. Next time, I will present the sense of closure provided by this form.

I will now examine with you three biblical instances of this chiasm, or arrow lines.

First, Matt 13 can be seen to exhibit two chiasmic structures. The diagrams below show how Jesus's giving of his reason for using parables falls at the apex of the arrow, giving Jesus's sermon here its "Aha!" moment. The repetition of the experience is for stronger impact.

Part 1

A. Parable of the sower (Matt 13:3–9)
    B. Invitation to hear (Matt 13:9)
        C. Reason for parables (Matt 13:10–17; Isa 6:6–9)
        C'. Hearing and seeing (Matt 13:14–17)
    B'. Invitation to hear (Matt 13:18)
A'. Parable of the sower explained (Matt 13:18–23)

Part 2

A. Another parable: tares and wheat (Matt 13:24–30)
    B. Another parable: mustard seed (Matt 13:31–32)
        C. Another parable: leaven (Matt 13:33)
            D. Reason for rarables (Matt 13:34–35; Ps 78:2)
        C'. Parable of the hidden treasure (Matt 13:44)
    B'. Parable of the costly Pparl (Matt 13:45–46)
A'. Parable of good and bad fish (Matt 13:47–50)

Table 03. Matt 13: Chiasm[1]

Second, Luke 9:51—19:48 is the central part of the Gospel of Luke. It is the famous journey motif, or odyssey form, that Luke used to tell the story of Jesus. I give you this diagram to help you see how the journey itself has the shape of a chiasm. The word at the center and the edges, "eschatological," is just another word built on a Greek word meaning last things, that is, last things in Jesus's life, last things for the disciples, last things that bring in the kingdom.

---

1. Terian, "Parables Discourse" (July 1, 1993).

Jesus's Journey, According to Luke

To Jerusalem: eschatological events (Luke 9:51–56)
  Follow me (Luke 9:57—10:12)
   What shall I do to inherit eternal life? (Luke 10:25–41)
    Prayer (Luke 11:1–13)
     Signs and the present kingdom (Luke 11:14–31)
      Conflict with the Pharisees: money (Luke 11:37—12:34)
       The kingdom is not yet and is now (Luke 12:35–59)
        The call of the kingdom to Israel (Luke 13:1–9)
         The nature of the kingdom (Luke 13:10–20)
          Jerusalem: eschatological events (Luke 13:22–35)
         The nature of the kingdom (Luke 14:1–11)
        The call of the kingdom to outcasts (Luke 14:12—15:32)
       The kingdom is not yet and is now (Luke 16:1–8, 16)
      Conflict with the Pharisees: money (Luke 16:9–31)
     Signs and the coming kingdom (Luke 17:11–37)
    Prayer (Luke 18:1–4)
   What shall I do to inherit eternal life? (Luke 18:18–30)
  Follow me (Luke 18:35—19:9)
To Jerusalem: eschatological events (Luke 19:10, 28–48)

Table 04. Jesus's Journey, According to Luke[2]

These chiastic structures in the Bible fascinate me. They have kept me studying for decades. I think and think about the meaning of the apex, the intersection, and about the use of mirror imagery to flank the "Aha!" at the apex.

One more, a fourth illustration, I bring from Scripture. This is more complicated because I want to show you how both Daniel and Revelation, in manifesting their parallel themes, also present chiastic structures.

---

2. Bailey, *Poet & Peasant*, 80–82.

Revelation, Compare with Daniel
A. 1–3 Churches: God knows and shows the future with promises A. 1–3 *Revelation* of Jesus (Rev 1:1)
B. 4–5 God is with us even in death B. 4–5 Jesus *in midst* of throne, *fire* burning before (Rev 5:6) **B. 4–5 Throne, to open the book (Rev 4:4–5; 5:1, 5, 11)**
C. 6–7 God is king on the throne among his people C. 6–7 Wipe tears from *eyes* (Rev 7:17)
D. 8–11 Trumpets: fall of a nation D. 8–11 Mystery of God *finished* (Rev 10:7)
E. 12 Dragon: deliverance at the end of the age E. 12 Stars/dragon *cast* down/out (Rev 12:4, 9–10)
F. 13 *Beasts* and *book* of life (Rev 13:1–8) **F. 13 Understanding (Rev 13:8)**
E'. 14 Three angels fly before the end E'. 14 Vine of earth *cast* in (Rev 14:19)
D'. 15–16 Plagues: fall of Babylon D'. 15–16 *Seventh* plague: it is *done* (Rev 16:17)
C'. 17–18 Lamb is Lord of lords and King of kings C'. 17–18 *Mourning* over Babylon, *weeping* (Rev 18:7–8)
B'. 19–20 God is with us, knight in white for battle B'. 19–20 Lake of *fire* (Rev 19:20–21; 20:10) **B'. 19–20 *Throne, books opened* (Rev 20:4, 11–12, 14)**
A'. 21–22 God knows and shows the fulfillment of promises A'. 21–22 Seal not this book. . . . It is done (Rev 21:6; 22:7, 10)

Table 05. Revelation

Daniel, Compare with Revelation
A. 1–2 God knows and shows political future A. 1–2 *Reveals* the future (Dan 2:12) **A. 1–2 *Understanding* (Dan 1:4)**
B. 3 God is with us in the furnace of trials B. 3 Jesus *in midst* of *fire* (Dan 3:25)
C. 4 God waits, Nebuchadnezzar takes God as king C. 4 King *lifts up* his *eyes* (Dan 4:34)
D. 5 Wall writing: fall of Babylon D. 5 Kingdom *finished* (Dan 5:26)
E. 6 Lions: Deliverance at the end of his life E. 6 Daniel, then accusers, *cast* in (Dan 6:16, 24)
F. 7 *Beasts* and *books* (Dan 7:3–21) F. 7 *Throne, books opened* (Dan 7:10)
E'. 8 Sanctuary cleansed at end of 2300 days E'. 8 Truth *cast* down (Dan 8:11–12)
D'. 9 Messiah: end of transgression D'. 9 *Seventy* weeks to *finish* (Dan 9:24)
C'. 10 God is King over the prince of Persia C'. 10 *Mourning* over vision, *lifts up* his *eyes* (Dan 10:2)
B'. 11 God is with us for strength and help in the great war B'. 11 Tried by *fire* (Dan 11:35)
A'. God knows and shows who is written in the book A'. *Seal* the *book*. . . . All these things *finished* (Dan 12:4, 7, 9) A'. Understanding (Dan 12:3–4, 8, 10)

Table 06. Daniel

This is the picture that enthralls, excites, and encourages me with no limit in sight. These are the "Aha!" insights in which I think I will always delight.

Arrow lines, opposites in proximity, can point the way to the beautiful and important things.

9

Returning Lines, Shapes

I HAVE BEEN WALKING in the woods in Wisconsin. The autumn-colored leaves lie all around me on the ground, most of them still moist in the chilly fog of the day. I am gathering the pretty ones and specimens of different shapes. I know the difference between white oak and red oak by the shape of their leaves, but the oaks have not yet granted me their leaves on the ground. What I have in my hand are brilliantly fired leaves from the maple tree shaped sort of like a hand with three fingers, yellow leaves from the elm tree shaped like a pointed Christmas tree light bulb with prickles, and a few yellow-and-brown spotted leaves from the poplar tree shaped like a fat heart. I take my collection inside, and my mother gets paper and crayons for us. We lay a leaf flat on the table and then the paper on top of the leaf. We color over the leaf on the paper, and yes—there it is, the shape of the leaf recorded right there on the paper.

In this chapter, I will discuss returning lines. A line that returns to its starting point yields a shape. The shape may be a leaf, a circle, a heart, a triangle, a butterfly wing, a quarter-moon, or a hand.

After the midday meal the adults sit around the farmhand-long table in the sunlit dining room of my grandparents' farmhouse. The adults like to talk or read a book together. I get restless. Pretty soon, the paper and crayons come out. One of my aunts draws a stereotypical cat shape for me and I try to copy. Then there is a fish shape, and a house, and a spruce tree. The one I like best is when someone draws around my hand. The touch of the crayon against my fingers pleases me, and I get to finish the picture by bringing the line full circle across the empty space where my wrist had lain.

Music knows this form, calling it ABA or AABA, returning to the beginning themes to finish the composition.

Let us discuss the concept in the Bible of coming full circle. In chapter 8, I introduced the structure called chiasm, and we explored the impact of the structure when it highlights a point of "Aha!," a turn in the story. Now I want to discuss chiasm as it impacts the pleasure of full-circle closure.

One illustration of coming full circle is the classic "Hangman Hanged" plot and story. In the Bible, Esther is perhaps the most obvious instance of this full-circle story.

Esther
A. Esther was a queen in Persia.
B. Esther's uncle, Mordecai, was an official in the palace and once had saved the king's life.
C. Haman was the highest official next to the king, hated Mordecai's loyalty to God, and built some gallows on which to hang Mordecai.
D. Esther bravely asked the king for help, and that night the king read the record of Mordecai's good deed.
C'. Haman was commanded to honor Mordecai on a tour through the city, then he was hung on his own gallows.
B'. Esther's uncle became the highest official and helped his people.
A'. Esther was a queen in Persia and beloved by her people.

Table 07. Esther: Reversal

A second illustration is as popular, the "Victorious Victim" plot and story. The story of Joseph in the Bible is a delicious instance of this full-circle story.

Joseph
A. Joseph was a favored son and had dreams of ruling his family.
B. His brothers sold him to slavery, and then on false accusation he landed in prison.
C. Joseph was blessed by God and could interpret dreams, which lifted him to a place next to Pharaoh.
B.' His brothers showed up and unknowingly bowed to their brother.
A.' Joseph could favor and save his brothers because he was ruler of the whole Egyptian Empire.

Table 08. Joseph: Reversal

A third illustration of coming full circle can be delightfully discovered in Matthew. The first name given to Jesus was Emmanuel, which means "God with us" (Matt 1:23), and the final words of Jesus, in fact, some of the final words in the book of Matthew, assert "I am with you always" (Matt 28:20 author paraphrase). This is a fine instance of envelope construction, and by using this construction, the author pulls me into the sense of closure, the assurance inside my very being, that indeed Jesus finished the work to make God's presence on earth a forever thing.

I believe this sense of full circle and closure is often communicated even subliminally by the very shape of the passage. The author revisits in reverse order everything he or she opened at first, and when the last door is closed, the reader feels satisfied. All his anticipations were dealt with, perhaps not as hoped or expected, but satisfyingly. I believe God wants humans to feel the truth as well as to know it intellectually. This is why he placed and preserved these forms and structures in the Bible to captivate human attention.

Please look at a fourth illustration with me. The book of Revelation is a thrilling instance of chiasm with its thorough full-circle closure. Please notice these verbal comparisons between beginning and ending.

Compare		
Rev 1:1	Rev 22:6	to show unto his servants
Rev 1:3	Rev 22:7, 10	blessed is he . . . time is at hand
Rev 1:8	Rev 22:6, 13	I am Alpha and Omega
Rev 1:11	Rev 22:18–19	write in a book
Rev 1:17	Rev 22:13	I am . . . the first and the last
Rev 2:7	Rev 22:2, 14, 19	tree of life
Rev 2:11	Rev 21:7	to the one who overcomes
Rev 2:11	Rev 20:6; 21:8	second death
Rev 2:16; 3:11	Rev 22:7, 12, 20	I come quickly
Rev 2:23	Rev 22:12	give . . . according to your works
Rev 2:28	Rev 22:16	morning star
Rev 3:5	Rev 21:27	book of life
Rev 3:12	Rev 21:2, 10	new Jerusalem, coming down
Rev 3:14	Rev 21:5; 22:6	faithful and true witness
Rev 3:21	Rev 21:5	to sit with me in my throne

Table 09. Revelation: Beginning and Ending

To gather my leaves, I go past the big oak tree that kept its leaves, past the elm tree by the barn, past the poplar stand by the swamp, and into the deeper woods where the stately maples stand. When I have gone far enough and gathered that which fills my hand, then I go out of the deep woods, past the poplar stand and the swamp, past the elm tree and the barn, and past the oak tree with its leaves still hanging on. Though I may be deep in thought, the very atmosphere of each beauty reaches back to the previous pass-by and lets me know I am nearer home at each step. When I reach the house, I have returned, not only with my feet and body but also in my emotions and attentions. Yes, I am different when I pass each beauty on the way back. For one thing, I now have a handful of color that I do not want to tear by grabbing a rock or tree with that hand. For another thing, I carry more pictures in my mind of the beauty around me.

I want for you the experience of having many pictures of beauty in your mind. I really do hope you will read the Bible for the beauty of it.

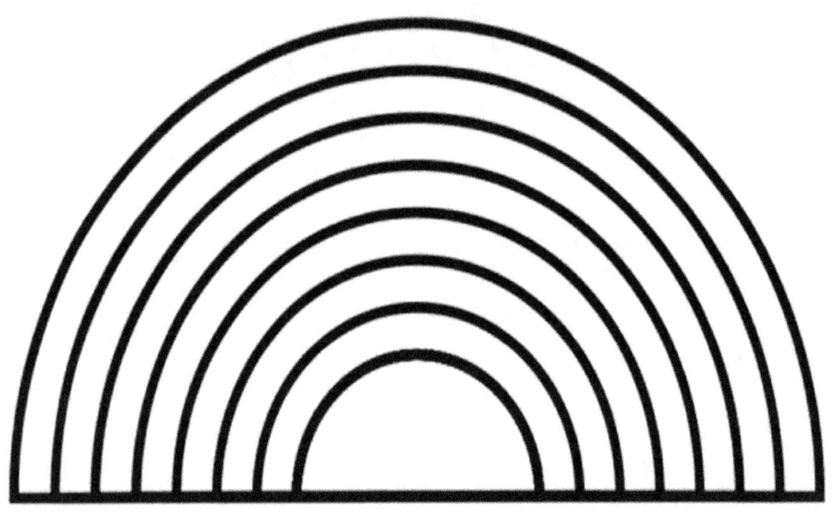

10

Color

I am waking in a small house in the Mississippi country. Spring is springing. Sun is rising. I open the back door to a scent I have never before experienced. I look up in awe, as in a child's wonder, to see something hanging like bunches of grapes all around the little stoop and space that separate me from the tree line. The scent is a bit spicy, like pumpkin pie mixed with the lilac fragrance I remember wafting into my open window years before in Wisconsin. It is not pumpkin pie season; it is not even lilac season. Now the sunlight streams through the trees lighting on the wisteria that has overnight made itself at home in my home. In the sunlight, I see one of my favorite colors gracing those blossoms that hang like bunches of grapes. Yes, the purple of wisteria is one color that draws me in. The year I was sixteen, I painted all my furniture that purple. I bought the paint, had it mixed to the exact tint, more violet than burgundy. I could look at that color forever, I think.

I chose the exact color for my eighth-grade graduation dress, and my mother made it for me. Chartreuse green is what we called it then. It is the green of the springtime, the warm and bright yellow-green that dresses most trees as the leaves burst into the new warmth of the increasing sunlight. The first time I knew that the color by itself, without all the other accoutrements of spring, could thrill my sight was when I saw a shirt by that color on an acquaintance. I astonished myself noticing the joy I felt while feasting my eyes on that color.

There is one more color that feeds my soul remarkably. I rise before sunrise to see this color in the sky. I suppose there are some bodies of water that show this color, and we would call it aqua. Since I have never lived by such a lake, I find the color in the predawn sky. This favorite color is not the one in the post-sunset sky. No, that color is different to me. The only reason I can postulate for that difference is that dusk sky is a time of receding light, and dawn sky is a time of approaching light. I could attribute my feelings about it to expectations of a new day versus confusions of a day passed. Yet, I think it is more than that for me. I think it is like the sound of an approaching train seems higher to the ear than the sound of the same train going away. The vibrations strike the ear slightly faster on approach and slightly slower on retreat. Perhaps the light striking the eye has a similar phenomenon. Whatever the reason, in the dawn there is a color of aqua that attracts my gaze for no other reason than the color.

Just as I have had trouble describing to you the colors I love, in the same way Bible authors struggled to describe the most beautiful things they had ever seen. As I turned to nature for description help, they described colors in terms of the jewels they knew. Let us look at a few of these scenes of awesome splendor, the throne of God and the city of God.

Moses and seventy-three other people saw God. Honest! It is recorded in Exod 24:9–10. I do not know that I have ever heard these verses highlighted from the pulpit, yet here they are. Under God's feet was something that looked like "paved work of a sapphire stone, and as it were the body of heaven in his clearness" (Exod 24:10). I understand sapphire has a blue color, but the word "sapphire" was not enough for this author; he had to add the sky to describe the wonder of that sight. I would have to look and look again, I think.

Ezekiel twice saw the sapphire-stone appearance of the throne of God (Ezek 1:26; 10:1). Ezekiel saw much more and did a courageous work to try to describe it. Let us let the mere descriptions of the colors involved pile up and rush over us in reading Ezek 1. What do you see when you read in Ezek 1:4, 27 "like the color of amber"? Probably some mix of yellow, orange, red, and brown. What do you see in Ezek 1:16 "like the color of a beryl"? The word has Greek origins, indicating blue-green and the color of seawater. Finally, I feel the overwhelm as the author gives up on color descriptions and merely claims a "brightness round about" (Ezek 1:27). Yet he could not leave it at that. He had to describe that brightness all around as like "the bow that is in the cloud in the day of rain" (Ezek 1:28). Apparently, this human was made to see all the colors of the rainbow in this light surrounding God's throne. In my mind's eye, I am looking all around me, slowly pivoting with mouth agape. I would stay here always.

The author of Revelation described his visit to the throne room of God using echoes from Ezekiel's description. We will study here only the colors in Rev 4:3. The colors of jasper and sardine stones would include the yellow-red-brown side of the spectrum, both being chalcedony. The rainbow here is green like an emerald.

The final picture of colors in the Bible describes a place where I want to stay forever. Go to Rev 21:18–20, please. The walls are of jasper, the city itself like pure gold, but the mineral gold does not do the color justice; the author had to add "like clear glass" (Rev 21:21 author paraphrase). Sit with me a minute with those colors. Can you picture them? I admit I am overwhelmed by the many jewels used to describe the colors of the twelve foundations of this city. I do not know the colors of those jewels that would have been known well enough to that author for him to use the jewels as description. What I do know is that there is color in the heavenly city, color enough to draw my attention and study for centuries, I think.

Will you join me in reading the Bible to discover the beauty in it?

11

Movement

It is a lazy day in the mountains of Colorado. I am lying on my back on a smooth rock, watching the float and swirl and purpose of a large hawk high above me, using the updrafts from the canyon to create amazingly beautiful movement. I cannot take my eyes from that bird. To me this is beauty, the way that bird moves.

I am lying on my couch in the family living room in Wisconsin, home from school with the mumps. My Chihuahua mix dog has put up with my fever and lethargy by sleeping right next to me all day for a couple of days. Now he senses I am a little better, probably because I have just slipped my hand under the covers and made a mole hump right in front of him. His eyes light up. His body tenses. His first pounce is merely a test. Then he wakes to full body involvement. His back legs bunch under his crouch. His ears stand straight up. His front legs dance to the bounce of my hump. This time his pounce includes a talkative growl and snapping teeth. Every part of his body is directed toward one end. Watching the movement and interacting with its focused intensity keeps me occupied and away from boredom during the several days of my recovery.

Movement in nature attracts and holds my attention. Picture the movement of flames in a campfire, of the water of a stream flowing over rocks, of clouds moving in the sunset or in front of a full moon. Movement is one of the elements of beauty in nature that has the power to captivate me.

Let us study a few instances of the beauty of movement in the Bible.

Matthew used the sermons of Jesus to move along the story in his Gospel. Matthew recorded a sermon and then wrote his clue to movement, "When Jesus had ended these sayings" or something similar (Matt 7:28; 11:1; 13:53; 19:1; 26:1). One can locate the sermons, and understand the movement, by finding this formula of words that marks the movement.

Luke used the journey idea to move along the story in his Gospel. Luke told some incidents in Jesus's life and then wrote his clue to movement, "Jesus went . . . journeying to Jerusalem" or something similar (Luke 9:51; 9:53; 13:22; 17:1; 18:31; 19:11; 19:28). This formula keeps the reader in tune with where the author is going and, of course, where Jesus is going too.

John organized his Gospel around signs to help people believe in Jesus. The English words "sign" and "miracle" both translate the one Greek word in this case. One could search for both of these words in the Gospel of John and discover the movement markers in his story. There is a "beginning of miracles," a popular clamoring for a sign, a "second miracle," and "many other signs" (John 2:11, 18, 23; 3:2; 4:48, 54; 6:2, 14, 26, 30; 7:31; 9:16; 10:41; 11:47; 12:18, 37; 20:30). The primary marker that stands as the clue to this movement is in John 20:31, where John told the purpose for choosing the stories he chose from among the many others. His purpose was that his readers might believe.

Now it is disclaimer time. I can hear someone responding with raised eyebrows or even a subtle smirk.

- "So they are just stories, aren't they! Different people retelling stories, leaving out some things, making the story spin to their own motives."

- "Hey, do you believe any of this really happened? Is it all just written to create a sense of movement and thereby some kind of beauty in literature?"

- "You want us to read for the beauty in the Bible. Seems like you're making too much emphasis on beauty and structure, so much that we'll overlook the message, the truths of the Bible!"

Yes, I believe everyone who tells the story of Jesus has to leave things out. There is too much. John even said the books it would require to tell it all would be so many as to overflow even the world itself (John 20:25). Yet I believe also that God willed that the story be told, limited as it must be by human capacity. This is why we need many people telling the story, many, many different expressions of the God event.

And yes, I do believe this all happened. I believe there are important truths in the Bible that we are required not to overlook. I believe the key truth is Jesus, the most beautiful Person who ever lived on this earth. I believe that Jesus and God ordained that the stories told about them should be beautiful in order to illustrate, and lead people to, the God we worship (see Ps 96:9). My call to read the Bible for the beauty in it is based on my belief that God will use whatever means he can to call us to himself, and if the beauty in the Bible captivates you, gaining for God more of your attention, then my purpose in the call has been accomplished. The caution is that we humans have some tendency to put the created thing in the place of the Creator in our affections. I warn all of us to let the beauty lead us to the God of beauty, and never let the beauty become an end in itself. More disclaimers in a future chapter.

For one last illustration of movement in the Bible, I present the sevens in Revelation. Look at Revelation 1:11; 5:1; 6:1; 8:2, 6; 16:1. There are many more instances of seven in this book, which you could find and research by yourself. I listed only those groups of seven that tell step by step what each individual in the seven entails. It was an "Aha!" moment for me when I flipped the axes on the chart in my head. I had been comparing the ones in all the sevens, and the twos, and the threes, etc. Now I began to see these sevens as mileposts or markers or clues to the movement or plot in Revelation.

Plot and Closure in Revelation and Daniel		
Introductions		
1.	Setting: evil vs. good; good in captivity	
	Rev 1	Rome vs. Jerusalem, John held captive by Rome
	Dan 1	Babylon vs. Jerusalem, Daniel taken captive by Babylon
2.	Characters: nations and denominations	
	Rev 2–3	"Seven churches" with promise for the church
	Dan 2	Great metal image of the nations
First Act		
3.	Oppressive nation attacks; Lamb delivers	
	Rev 4–5	Lamb to the rescue
	Dan 3	Nation against Daniel
4.	Lamb's kingdom expands	
	Rev 6–7	Lamb opens "seven seals" of a book
	Dan 4	King converted
5.	Oppressive nation meets its ruin	
	Rev 8–11	"Seven trumpets" bring ruin to nations
	Dan 5	Fall of Babylon
Central Act		
6.	Devil attacks	
	Rev 12	Devil against Jesus and God's people
	Dan 6	Another nation against Daniel
7.	Whole world decrees against God	
	Rev 13	Four nations and an evil decree
	Dan 7	Four nations and the judgment
8.	God gets a hearing	
	Rev 14	Three angels shout for God in the sky
	Dan 8	God vindicated in court
Last Act		
9.	God announces deliverance	
	Rev 15–16	"Seven plagues" bring ruin to Babylon
	Dan 9	Angel announces Messiah's coming
10.	End of false worship systems	
	Rev 17–18	Seven laments describe Babylon's ruin
	Dan 10	Daniel describes his angel experience
11.	Devil's last stand	
	Rev 19–20	Lamb rides the skies; devil attacks and dies
	Dan 11	Great war with willful kings
Triumphant Conclusion		
12.	New setting: good on the throne	
	Rev 21–22	Good people rule a world of promise
	Dan 12	Good prince stands up for his people

Table 10. Revelation and Daniel: Plot and Closure

You see, however God keeps me focused on the word, whatever God uses to keep me totally engrossed in Godself, I welcome and happily pursue. I invite you to find something that will keep you reading the Bible, not to prove anything or to gather trivia for conversation but to come into connection with the mind of God, to bathe your thoughts and affections in divine thought.

12

Depth

I AM WALKING HOME from school in Wisconsin. Today was the first day of school this year, and right now the walk home has gotten hot. I am walking along the fencerow of a pasture where a few yards away the woods begins. Looking at the cool shade under those woods, and the green carpet underneath, I long to follow after the cows who gather there. I have had this longing many times, even while riding along through the countryside. I see a welcoming pastoral scene, and I think I could just get out of the car and wrap that pastoral picture right around me. It does not work that way. Sometimes we stop the car and go walking into the scene, and then the scene disappears as I watch my step around cow hillocks or protruding rocks that I did not notice from the road. I can revel in the depth and perspective from a distance, and when I step into the picture, I lose that perspective.

I have been practicing my flute now for a few years. This springtime I am determined to try to discover the robin's song and play it on my flute. I listen and listen. The robin's song does not yield its secrets quickly to my ear. I ask my teachers, and no one offers a music score or even an explanation for why there is no music score. A couple of years after the start of this quest, I ask one of the real musicians among my school friends, and he suggests that perhaps the robin's song is full of many more frequencies than we can distinguish. I find a book in the school library (title long forgotten now) that shows pictures of the sound frequencies in birds' songs. Yes, indeed, the robin and the meadowlark have deeply complex songs. I think I will return to mere listening. From a distance, the depth and perspective of the robin's song does enwrap me in its magic.

Depth, with perspective, is another element in beauty that draws me in. I didn't know what was wrong with my pictures until an artist assigned me to draw a temple. He wanted a round gazebo-like structure with seven pillars. I tried, but it was really not good. Then he showed me how the pillars at the back of the circle of pillars must be slightly thinner than the pillars nearer the viewer. This made an enormous difference in my satisfaction level with my art. He taught me how to try to achieve the sense of depth and perspective in my work.

I am drawing at my desk in school in Wisconsin. I am in sixth grade, and since all my schoolwork is finished, with As, and since none of the other students are clamoring for my tutoring at the moment, I am drawing. It is a cricket. Anyone who drops by can see it is a cricket. It is a cricket from an ant's perspective. The insect fills the page and even kicks off the page with its hind legs. The grass in which it "hides" runs off the top of the page. It is a cricket from a ground-level perspective.

Wherever I stand, I see things from a particular and specific perspective, and I can discover depth. Yet sometimes it helps to stand back, get some distance, see the bigger picture, and not let the view of a hillock of grass, or a cricket, eclipse the view of the woods with its green carpet or something even bigger.

I am discussing in this section the idea of depth and perspective in the Bible. The front and center proposition is that Christ is its focal point. All other beauty in the Bible wraps around, directs the eye to, gives perspective to, Jesus and the event of his entrance and impact in this world. This is why sometimes in my reading, I look away and see the big picture, with Jesus and his love as my only and forever attraction.

There are two other ways I suggest of stepping back to view the beauty of the Bible in its bigger picture.

Someone once said that any book deserves to be read all the way through. The more I have read, the more I believe that. This is how I read. I prefer to set myself to reading one book of the Bible or one author's set of books. I will read this set over and over until its big picture seeps into my soul, until I start fitting every little piece into a larger context. Students who attend my classes know that one of my first rules is "check the context." Reading and rereading a chosen book or set of books will help give you a sense also of the historical setting of the message. I encourage researching the historical setting in reliable sources and then returning to the Bible itself for reading in context. This is my way of gaining depth and perspective in my Bible reading.

Second, I recommend reading the Bible through as it is, the whole Bible. Some people do this each year. Reading and rereading the whole Bible discovers a general context for each part and each proposition. It puts each truth in its perspective as God preserved it for us in his word. I also recommend reading the Bible in chronological order. You can find my choice of order in appendix A, "Chronological Story Order for Reading the Books of the Bible." Read one whole book of the Bible at a time, and then read all the books in order according to their storyline. This way, even the puzzling books, like some of the minor prophets, slip more easily into place in the bigger picture.

We are looking for depth of understanding, breadth of perspective, beauty that captivates.

13

Sound Articulation

I AM PULLING WEEDS in our family garden. My mother is working a row over from me, and my small dog is probably down the road visiting his wished-for girlfriend. The sun is hot on our backs; the air is still. A western meadowlark takes a stand on a nearby fence-post. I cannot help but stand up and look when that bird lets out its song. The tones are full throated, well rounded, and arresting in their beauty. Pretty soon my mother urges me back to the task at hand, my dog comes trotting back with tongue hanging out, and I catalog the sound of the meadowlark as part of the context for my upbringing.

I have been practicing the organ for an hour and will begin flute practice next. I look out the big window to see the cows coming in from the woods across the street. Their udders are full, and some of them stop to low and then move on. The moo is a bellow sometimes rising in pitch a bit throughout its extenuated sounding. The cows' moos are also part of the context for my upbringing. I return to practicing my flute, always hunting for the sound from my instruments that makes me happy and speaks to me of beauty.

Sound is made by vibration. It seems the meadowlark's whole body vibrates, yet it is primarily its tongue and throat vibrations that make the sound. The cow involves its whole body also, with something in its throat most active. In the flute, it is the column of air in the barrel that vibrates. If I had a real pipe organ, it would be the air inside the pipes that vibrates. On the piano or violin, it is the strings. On the drum, it is the membrane and the air inside. On my brother's saxophone, it is the reed and the air around it. A musician grows so close to his or her instrument that it is the experience of the vibrations that thrills the performer and inspires what he or she will do next.

The performer can affect the sound primarily by what we call articulation, how the sound is initiated and terminated. Various kinds of articulation include short, disconnected, smooth, connected, loud, soft, accented, slower, faster, and attenuated. It is the combination of these within a sensitive performer that can pull the audience into the message of that music according to that performer. There are any number of articulation combinations.

To show you something about articulation in the Bible, I will use Jesus's seven short sayings from the cross, as we have them recorded in the Gospels.

From Luke 23:34, we have "Father, forgive them; for they know not what they do." In your ears, how is this articulated? In a whisper, between beats of the hammer driving in the nails? Or in a commanding voice though broken by throbs of pain?

From John 19:26–27, we hear "Woman, behold your son! . . . Behold your mother!" Are these private words, smooth and connected in their compassion and love? Or are they squeezed out disconnectedly in brokenness?

From Luke 23:43 (author paraphrase) comes the promise "Surely I tell you today, you will be with me in paradise." There must have been some slight lift in Jesus's spirits in finding that someone trusted him, on that day of all days, and in knowing that he really could promise something out of this world in response to the trust expressed. I wonder if there was a little more breath for this saying, a little more connectedness, a little more accent on what meant the most to him.

From Matt 27:46 and Mark 15:34, we hear the saying "My God, my God, why have you forsaken me?" Both Matthew and Mark described what was heard as a "loud voice." Was it disconnected for breath between bursts? Or was it one attenuated bellow of unmitigated anguish?

From John 19:28, we hear "I'm thirsty." I think perhaps it was a short, accented call to the humans around the cross. Considering all the blood he had lost, of course, he would be thirsty beyond all measure.

From John 19:30 comes "It is finished." John wrote about a loud voice for these words, and these are the very last words according to John. Finished means completed, brought to full fruition, the end. Here Jesus's light went out with a shout of victory.

From Luke 23:46, we can hear "Father, into thy hands I commend my spirit," as Jesus's final intimate moment with a Father whose face was still hidden. For Luke, Jesus died in quiet surrender, in a simple letting go of the sound.

The articulation of events in Scripture helps us move with the story, and yet not all is given us in the writing. We have room to imagine the articulation of the words. Come back and read it again; you might hear a different articulation the next time.

14

Sound Overtones

My brother and I are gathered around our mother in the kitchen. She has a matchbox in her hand without its slide-on cover. She puts a couple rubber bands around the box so they cross over the open side of the box. Then she shows us how to pluck the rubber bands to make a new kind of sound. The rubber bands vibrate.

One evening, my father sends us to the button box to get a big button. We return with a coat button that he says will do, though he wishes it were bigger. He threads about four feet of string through two of its holes and ties together the string's ends, to get a continuous band of string. He takes hold of the string with both hands about two feet apart with the button dangling on the string between his hands. He starts the button swinging until he has a button spinner. It makes a buzzing sound.

I want to use this toy to explain harmonics, about which I learned much later. The entire length of the string was buzzing one sound. The string from the button to my father's hand was buzzing another sound. Half of the half of the string was buzzing another sound. And half of the half of the half was buzzing another sound. This overtone halving goes on infinitely.

Take this to the violin or piano string. The entire length of the string vibrates, and while that is happening there is a secondary vibration that takes up each half-length of the string. While those two vibrations are sounding, there is a tertiary vibration that takes up each quarter-length of the string. This division of string length and multiplication of sound keeps happening infinitesimally though we cannot hear it all. These extra sounds are called overtones or harmonics, and they add richness to the sound.

Healthy, strong vocal cords produce harmonics. The air in the barrel of a flute or saxophone produces harmonics. The membrane and air in a drum produce harmonics. Harmonics is one thing that keeps performers coming back and back to the music. It is what makes you love a certain person's voice. People have noticed this for centuries, and much music has been written in beautiful "thirds."

Harmonics is the reason also that I very much like the sound of two voices singing at the interval of a third. This interval is the second strongest overtone, and someone who sings at that interval from another voice makes music that is extremely pleasing to me.

I will suggest here that one place harmonics happen in the Bible is in the old poetry parallelisms. Bible poetry is not necessarily based on meter or rhyme. Much of the time it depends on synonymous or antonymous phrases, or completion phrases, in sets usually of two or three. There is the first phrase, then another as the first overtone. If there is a third phrase, it is the second overtone. Look at the first psalm, where each initial line is related to one or two following lines.

> Blessed is the one who walks not in counsel from the ungodly,
>> Nor stands where sinners stand,
>>> Nor sits in the scorner's seat.
> This person delights in the law of the Lord,
>> And in his law meditates day and night.
> He or she will be like a tree planted by the river,
>> Bearing fruit in season,
> This person's leaf will not wither,
>> And whatever he or she does will prosper.
>> (Ps 1:1–3 author paraphrase)

This kind of poetry translates much more effectively than that which depends on meter or rhyme. It is a poetry of thought. It builds thought on thought for a momentum that is powerful to the poet's purpose.

Not only in material recognized as poetry are overtones at work. Mark enjoyed putting double and triple phrases together in his Gospel. Look at these:

> The beginning of the gospel of Jesus Christ,
>   the Son of God. (Mark 1:1)

> Peace,
>   be still. (Mark 3:39a)

> And the wind ceased,
>   and there was a great calm. (Mark 3:39b)

> Lord, I believe;
>   help thou mine unbelief. (Mark 9:24)

Overtones, or harmonics, fill the sounds of ancient poetry in the Bible with richness, expansion, and joy. Let the Bible's sounds thrill you again and again.

15

Sound Resonance

I FINISH MY CHORES and go to nap time as my mother has directed. I miss my brother, who is old enough to go to school and every morning leaves me behind. I like to have the music going as I fall asleep. My parents have a reel-to-reel recording of a man with a resonant baritone voice singing some of the classical religious solos. I play to the music. I nap to the music. I do my chores to the music. Whenever the tape runs out, I ask my mother to start it again. I think it is that beautiful.

I am standing in the back of my pickup truck, preaching my heart out. I have a voice that carries far. My parents used to remind me not to sing or talk too loudly because I could be heard far away and over above the other children. Sometimes now that kind of voice is helpful. That which I find most fulfilling, but practice only when no one is around, is to sing in a large, closed space where the very air resonates with the sound of my voice. The shower or the car works, but an old, large church or cathedral is better. The human voice in resonance is one sound that is most captivating to me.

If not damped in some way, a string or membrane will vibrate in sympathy with another string that is set to vibrating and has the same or divisible vibration frequency. When you play a single note on the piano with the damper pedal down, many other strings sound along with the one you struck. This sympathetic vibration is called resonance.

Resonance and harmonics bring joy to the musician artist, somewhat the same as when someone's comments "resonate" with you and you feel a sense of connection and being understood. This joy in resonance and harmonics is important as both goal and reward to musicians.

One set of human vocal cords can produce vibrations that could be called harmonics, and those vibrations setting the air vibrating in the hollow spaces in the mouth and nose is called resonance. We might say such and such a person's voice has great resonance; it is pleasant to listen to.

In a church sanctuary or concert hall, one must consider further resonances and harmonics. The space in the main hall is filled with air like the barrel of a flute. It vibrates in resonance, and with its own harmonics. That is why choirs find joy in singing in the great cathedrals where the rooms are alive with resonance and harmonics.

I bring three illustrations of resonance in the Bible, and you will find many more.

As a child, I memorized Luke 2:52, the beloved passage about Jesus increasing in "wisdom and stature, and in favor with God and man." Sometime later I discovered its counterpart in the Old Testament, "Samuel grew on, and was in favor both with the Lord, and also with men" (1 Sam 2:26). Somehow for me, recognizing their resonance together brought both stories closer to my fondness and affections.

I am reading in Isa 6 the story of Isaiah's vision of God during which he confessed his sinfulness and then was prepared and called to his prophetic mission. I read of the angels around God's throne singing, "Holy, holy, holy is the Lord" (Isa 6:3). I wonder if threefold repetition is meant to convey the idea of echo or resonance, the sounds of their praise repeating and growing in glory. Then I sense another resonance rising in myself with the memory of hearing this same song in a different part of the Bible, "Holy, holy, holy is the Lord" (Rev 4:8). It is as if the whole Bible has become a resonance chamber to augment the marvelous praise. Then I start hearing in my mind the hymn by that name,[1] and my joy is enhanced yet again. Some people make notes in the margins of their Bibles to point to resonant passages.

The third illustration was just as striking to me. It was the recognition, when I read in Jeremiah about the covenant—that is, God's promise to cleanse our hearts and give us new hearts and write his law in our hearts—that I had heard very similar wording in Ezekiel and in Hebrews (Jer 31:3, 31–33; 32:37–40; Ezek 11:19–20; 36:25–28; Heb 8:13–18; 10:16). It seemed to me that the sound of the rainbow of promise had resonated all the way through Israel's darkest days and into the New Testament. It is still resonating in the promises, ready for us to let God make spaces in our hearts for his praise to resonate to his glory.

It is not wrong to find pleasure in reading the Bible, in hearing the resonances that reach far back into God's chambers. I believe God takes pleasure in our pleasure in this.

1. Heber, "Holy, Holy, Holy!"

16

Fragrance

I AM GOING ABOUT my work, minding my own business, when suddenly I think I see or feel a lightness. I have been deeply depressed for years, see no light at the end of the tunnel, and drag myself through the days with scant physical or mental energy. Then suddenly now something whisks by me and touches me slightly. I cannot see the thing. I sense it only after it is gone. Yet I know I have received a gift of some sort that leads or points me toward life. I have been working hard in therapy, sorting through some not useful thinking habits, changing how I look at many things, yet progress seems like slogging through black mud on a black night. And suddenly now this whiff catches my attention. I tell my therapist, "If that whatever-it-was is real, then I could want to live."

That was years ago for me, and I now believe the catalyst was my sense of smell reactivating, bringing back memories, influencing and activating my brain. As a child I loved the fragrance of lilacs, apple blossoms, and new-mown hay. In my adulthood I have added a joy in the fragrance of wisteria, mimosa, and the more delicate whiffs of kudzu in the fall and the first pine pollen in the spring. I have a friend who believes she sometimes smells God's presence as a fragrance unlike anything of earth.

Since fragrance seems important in connecting with beauty and God, let me show you how some fragrances might work in Bible reading. I read the Bible for many reasons: to teach a class, to preach the word in the pulpit and on the street, to research for writing, and to suggest an answer when someone asks me about a biblical topic. I know, however, that my most important reading of the Bible is a daily sitting with the assigned passage from a curriculum I have chosen for myself. I read, ponder, reread, write three pages, re-ponder, choose the brightest—and newest—spot of that work, and write four lines about it. I give myself only three or four lines to capture this whiff of God that will get away if I fail to put it into my own words and tell someone. I will show you a few of my whiffs of God from recent weeks:

- Sometime in my youth, I was astounded to learn that every day of my life would be simply keeping on in Christ the way I began, repenting, confessing, trusting, and accepting, with never a day in which I would not need repentance. This is still my hope and courage (Col 2:1–29).

- Rather than merely a plea to be heard, Ps 120 is a testimony that God did hear. Our God is a listening God. That is why, as the psalm goes on to say, lying lips and a deceitful tongue are so disastrous and things from which to be delivered.

- For two hundred years there had been no Passover in Jerusalem until King Hezekiah called for one. There was much repenting and great joy. The last verse says their prayers *came* up to heaven, not their prayers *went* up to heaven, as I expected. Interesting perspective (2 Chron 30:1–27).

- The leader tried to paint it as a "simple" question of individual rights versus the common good. But when it was about Jesus, the individual was the only one who could save the common good. My gratitude and praise are that one man did die for the nation (John 11:47–57).

- I find it interesting that the authors who wrote in new covenant language (new heart, new spirit, for the inner writing of God's law) each wrote twice along those lines. Twice makes it sure and urgent (Jer 31:3, 31–33; 32:37–40; Ezek 11:19–20; 36:25–28; Heb 8:13–18; 10:16).

- Satan digs a pit in front of me, into which he himself falls. This is the story of God's victory in the universe, and it can be my story. Praises be to God (Ps 57).

- They were ignorant of the way to righteousness and tried to make themselves good by keeping the law. How often I simply forget what I know and try to use human rules and opinions to make me good. Trusting Jesus is the only way (Rom 10:1–4, 16–21)!

I invite you into Bible reading for the beauty of it, for the fragrance available, and for the reason to live that it can activate in us.

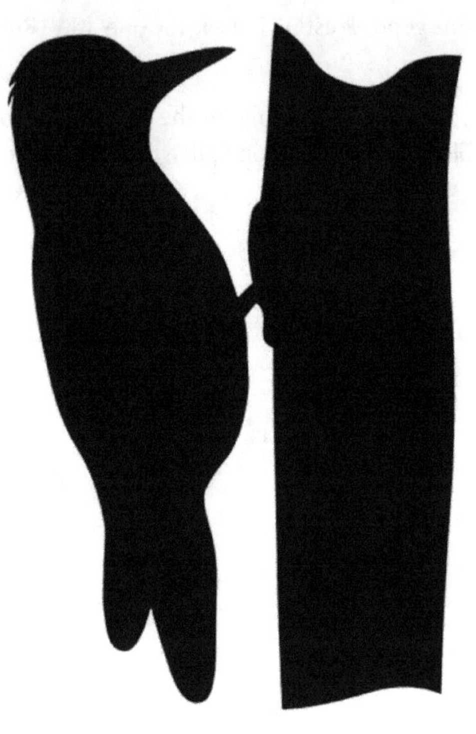

17

Function

I AM WATCHING A hummingbird at the feeder in the foothills of Colorado. His bill is like a small pipette ready to disturb the blossoms not at all while sucking up his nourishment. His wings in flight sound like a tiny helicopter, but here at the feeder they are almost silent as they keep his body still, hanging in midair. What fascinates me right now is that he does not have to fly at the feeder each time to get his bill deep inside. His body remains in one place while his head bobs to get his bill in and out for sucking and then swallowing. Every structure of that bird is appropriate for his function.

I am watching a woodpecker on a telephone pole in Georgia. If I banged my face against a tree that hard and long, I would surely have a bad headache. Instead, this bird's bill is made to penetrate, and his head is made to act like a hammer head. His feet are certainly more powerfully tenacious than my feet or hands could ever be, since they and his tail are required to provide stability for the hammer action. Again, what fascinates me most is that his neck does all the action, while the rest of his body remains tightly still. Every structure of this bird supports his function.

Inspired by a note made by Leonardo da Vinci, his biographer Walter Isaacson researched and described the tongue of a woodpecker, which must reach through the long beak far into, and up and down inside, the hole in the tree to find the insects and grubs. The tongue is so long that, when not foraging, "it retracts into the skull and its cartilage-like structure continues past the jaw to wrap around the bird's head and then curve down to its nostril." This arrangement cushions and shields the bird's brain from terrible shock during pecking.[1]

In this chapter, I will spend a few minutes in wonder over how the Bible's form and structure supports its function. I would like to study function on two levels: the human authors' intentioned function in use of that form, and God's intended function for his word. I have some problems with this stated goal. First, the human authors are dead, and I cannot ask them about their intentions. Second, I have no illusion that I, as human, can interview God for the depths of God's intention. I am handicapped. Yet, since the fit of form and function is another element of beauty as I find it in nature and the Bible, I am driven to comment here in meager patches of understanding.

Actually, throughout this book, I have been showing you the marvelous effects of each form on my understanding thorough various instances and Bible references. Here then are some concluding observations regarding form and function in the Bible.

- My first aim has been to entice you to read the Bible more, willing to bathe in its beauty rather than insisting on bottling some portion to prove or remember a point.

- I do believe the human authors could have understood the forms mentioned in this book and purposefully used them to illuminate the themes of their work.

- I believe that much of the power of the various forms we studied can be passed to the reader without his or her conscious knowledge of the forms. The power of the form works whether or not the form is recognized.

- I believe that God had a hand in the formation and preservation of the Bible, and some choices of form were divine.

1. Isaacson, *Leonardo da Vinci*, 524.

- An author could have chosen the form for writing, as the authors of the four Gospels each chose a different artistic form, or God could have chosen the form for the doing, as parts of Genesis and Revelation claim to be the simple record of God's artistic actions.

- As a painter intentionally structures his or her piece in order to direct the viewer's eyes on a path or to the focal point, and that direction often happens subliminally, in the same way, I believe these forms direct the reader's mind toward what the author or Author wanted humans to see.

- Of course, the stated themes of an author's work, and of the Bible as larger context, will for me always inform the study of form and structure.

- If I let my mind connect in delight with the forms for a while, I believe the more overtly stated themes will seep into my identity, perhaps subliminally while my conscious attention is captivated.

- Because I believe the stated themes of Scripture are the goodness of God and the worthiness of Christ, any Bible form or structure that points to God and his Christ, attracting and holding my attention and homage, would be worth my study and use.

- Finally, it seems to me that one of God's intentions was preservation and translation of the Bible over many years and into many languages. For that translation into many languages, the forms that we have addressed in this book are by far the best fit to bring into any language the beauty in the Bible.

Therefore, I lift up this Bible, I hold it out to you, I invite you with joy into its pages and stories and artistic forms. Will you read it and let it thrill you as it does me?

FAQs and Final Lines

I did enjoy visiting with you over this idea of reading the Bible for the beauty in it. During the writing and before, certain questions have come to me from various people who are thinking along with me. I am indebted to those friends who will follow my presentation and give feedback. My purpose in these seventeen chapters on beauty in the Bible is to invite you into reading the Bible in another way, in order to bathe your mind and heart in the presence of the God of beauty. Here are some hindrances and objections I have heard to reading the Bible for the beauty in it.

I AM AFRAID I WILL NOT GET IT RIGHT.

You are reading not to get it right but to connect with God. Contact with God *is* right!

SO-AND-SO DOES NOT GET IT RIGHT.

It is imperative that I maintain a good amount of humility on this. I am not God. I am not the one with whom someone else is connecting in the word of God. Therefore, it is not my job to make sure someone else gets it right.

WHAT WILL KEEP ME FROM MISLEADING SOMEONE ELSE?

I-language. I invite all of us to talk carefully about the Bible, to share our insights in I-language, recognizing our own inability to read the Bible for someone else, guarding against hubris, and cultivating humility here.

WHAT WILL CONTROL AGAINST MAVERICKS TAKING OVER THE INTERPRETATION OF SCRIPTURE FOR EVIL PURPOSES?

You and I being in the word for ourselves is our greatest defense against deception. If you would like a more detailed list of controls for inductive Bible reading, please go to appendix B, "Controls for Inductive Reading of the Bible."

I DO NOT WANT TO THINK OF THE BIBLE AS ART, BECAUSE THAT WOULD INDICATE TO ME THAT IT IS ALL MADE UP AND DID NOT REALLY HAPPEN.

I understand. Some of us have the same problem with thinking of the Bible as story, or as history, or as using sources. Too many have publicly argued that the Bible is "only" story, or "totally" a product of its own historical context, or "just" a compilation. As a result, now when I mention one of those things, someone automatically inserts "only" or "totally" or "just." Do not do that. The Bible is story; it is a product of its own historical context; it is a many-layered compilation with commentary. And the Bible is art! Yes, I do believe it really did happen and is not "just" made up. The authors who saw it happen felt free to shape the material, and the records that were artistic survived. Furthermore, I would say that God, being a God of beauty, felt free to shape the events and let the authors write what they saw, already shaped into beauty. Let us read the Bible! For more encouragement to read the Bible, see appendix C, "Fifteen Reasons Why I Read the Bible."

I AM CONCERNED THAT THIS EMPHASIS ON BEAUTY IN THE BIBLE ENCOURAGES THE WORSHIP OF THE CREATED THING INSTEAD OF THE CREATOR.

In my opinion, this is a very serious matter and must be examined every day of our lives. It would be possible to make Bible study for any reason into a false worship. Looking for proofs of truth, digging around in history, or even a daily Bible reading plan could lead me into idolatry. If I trust in anything before or besides God and his Christ for my entrance into heaven above or for health and happiness here on earth, I am thereby breaking the first commandment, sinning, breaking God's law. It is serious. Now switch gears, please. For those of us who long for that first commandment in our lives, that intimacy with God that will keep him in first place, there are a few things that can help us along. We can pray to God, including both talking and listening. We can gather and interact with fellow believers. We can cultivate solitude and silence and service and mindful living. And we can read the Bible. I extend this invitation to read the Bible for the beauty in it as one help, a powerful help, toward intimacy with the God of beauty. Ask him to guard you from idolatry as you study. He will.

BY THIS INVITATION TO READ THE BIBLE FOR THE BEAUTY IN IT, DO YOU REJECT CRITICAL BIBLICAL SCHOLARSHIP?

No, I do not.[1] Biblical criticism of the late nineteenth and early twentieth centuries brought much insight and understanding that was overlooked or even repressed earlier. In my opinion, historical criticism, source criticism, and text criticism called attention

1. Zalabak, "Toward 'Diversity in Cooperation.'"

to important pieces of biblical data. More recently there are trends in biblical scholarship toward putting the text back together, as it were, toward studying the text as it stands before us now, toward hearing the stories as whole stories. We can do this now with better insights because of those who produced the previous works. I continue to champion your reading of the Bible as it landed in your lap or on your desk, in whichever translation is accessible to you, and in many versions if you can.

My final appeal in this book is this: read the Bible! Be reading the Bible every day. Let it saturate your thinking. Let divine thought shape your mind.

The shape of divine thought is beauty.

Appendix A

Chronological Story Order for Reading the Books of the Bible

OLD TESTAMENT STORY ORDER

Genesis

Job

Exodus, Leviticus, Numbers, Deuteronomy

Joshua

Judges, Ruth

1 Samuel, Psalms 1–72

2 Samuel, 1 Chronicles, Psalms 73–150

1 Kings, Proverbs, Ecclesiastes, Song of Solomon

2 Kings, 2 Chronicles

Isaiah, Hosea, Amos, Jonah, Micah

Jeremiah, Lamentations, Nahum, Habakkuk, Zephaniah

Ezekiel, Daniel, Obadiah, Haggai, Zechariah

Ezra, Nehemiah, Malachi

Joel

Esther

NEW TESTAMENT STORY ORDER

Matthew, Mark, Luke, John

Acts

1 & 2 Thessalonians, 1 & 2 Corinthians, Galatians

Romans, Colossians, Philemon, Ephesians, Philippians

1 & 2 Timothy, Titus

James

1 & 2 Peter, Jude

Hebrews

1, 2, & 3 John

Revelation

APPENDIX B

Controls for Inductive Reading of the Bible

SINCE I AM ASKING you to read inductively, or experimentally, I will also present some controls for the experiment. I have chosen two controls, and these controls color my teaching and conversations about the Bible.

1. The first control for this study is surrender, a surrender that readily says, "I admit I do not have all the answers."
2. The second control for this study is context.
    a. Historical context
        i. The historical setting of the original writing and reading of the material
        ii. The history of its interpretation through the centuries
        iii. Since none of us knows all the historical context, at least the following realization is needed along with the humility it requires: "This was not written primarily for me and my time; I am overhearing it."
    b. Biblical context
        i. The chapter and chapters nearby are context for any verse(es).

ii.   The plot of each book is context for any part of that book.

iii.   The set of books written by any one author is context for any part of that set.

iv.   The entire Bible is context for any part of it.

v.   It follows then that the re-reader, having been exposed perhaps many times to the context's larger picture, has the edge in understanding.

Fifteen Reasons Why
I Read the Bible

1. To spend time with a Friend
2. To listen to a Friend
3. To connect with a Friend
4. To bathe my mind in divine thought
5. To satisfy my soul with beauty
6. To instill positive thinking and loving
7. To announce visually my allegiance to God
8. To turn the devil away
9. To signal to the universe whose side I am on
10. To gather ideas to use in prayer
11. To collect words by which to share my hope and joy
12. To become a storyteller
13. To expand my thinking
14. To sort out what I believe
15. To keep myself honest and avoid lies

Bibliography

Aland, Kurt, et al., eds. *The Greek New Testament.* New York: United Bible Societies, 1975.

Alter, Robert. *The World of Biblical Literature.* New York: Basic, 1992.

Bailey, Kenneth E. *"Poet & Peasant" and "Through Peasant Eyes": A Literary-Cultural Approach to the Parables in Luke, Combined Edition.* 1976. Reprint, Grand Rapids: Eerdmans, 1980.

Bernstein, Leonard. *The Infinite Variety of Music.* 1966. Reprint, New York: Leonard, 1993.

Brenton, Lancelot C. L., trans. *The Septuagint with Apocrypha: Greek and English.* London: Bagster, 1851.

Craddock, Fred B. *Craddock on the Craft of Preaching.* St. Louis: Chalice, 2011.

———. *Overhearing the Gospel.* St. Louis: Chalice, 2002.

Heber, Reginald. "Holy, Holy, Holy!" In *The Christian Life Hymnal*, edited by Eric Wyse, #1. Peabody, MA: Hendrickson, 2006.

Hillerman, Tony. *Dance Hall of the Dead.* New York: Harper, 1973.

Isaacson, Walter. *Leonardo da Vinci.* New York: Simon & Schuster, 2017.

Jourdain, Robert. *Music, the Brain, and Ecstasy: How Music Captures Our Imagination.* New York: HarperCollins, 1997.

Lee, Margaret E., and Bernard Brandon Scott. *Sound Mapping the New Testament.* Salem, OR: Polebridge, 2009.

Peterson, Eugene H. *Leap Over a Wall: Earthy Spirituality for Everyday Christians.* San Francisco: Harper, 1997.

Terian, Abraham. "Parables Discourse: Matt 13." Lecture for the course Gospels: Matthew, at Andrews University, Berrien Springs, MI, June–July, 1993.

White, Ellen G. *Steps to Crist.* Washington, DC: Review and Herald, 1982.

Zalabak, Wilma. "Toward 'Diversity in Cooperation': A Response to Blazen, Larson, and Mashchak." *Adventist Today* 4 (1996) 14–15.

www.ingramcontent.com/pod-product-compliance
Lightning Source LLC
Chambersburg PA
CBHW070738030726

47601CB00001B/60

Two Minute SQL Server Stumpers

Vol. 5

Brought to you by the staff at
SQLServerCentral.com

And

Red Gate Software

Thanks to the following for contributing
questions:

Chad Crawford
Sriram Yaddanapudi
Vincent Rainardi
Jacob Sebastian
Brandie Tarvin
Ramesh Saive
Carlos Iglesias Martinez
Surendra Holambe
Prashant Pandey
Reza Nassabeh
Gogula Aryalingam
Kenneth Fisher
and
VM and Abhijit

Red Gate Books
Newnham House
Cambridge Business Park
Cambridge
CB4 0WZ
United Kingdom

ISBN 978-1-906434-21-2

Disclaimer

Red Gate Books, SQLServerCentral.com, and the authors of the articles contained in this book are not liable for any problems resulting from the use of techniques, source code, or compiled executables referenced in this book. Users should review all procedures carefully, test first on a non-production server, and always have good backup before using on a production server.

Trademarks

Trademarked names may appear in this book. Rather than use a trademark symbol with every occurrence of a trademarked name, we use the names only in an editorial fashion and to the benefit of the trademark owner, with no intention of infringement of the trademark.